Belgian Sheepdogs

Marge Turnquist

Alpine Blue Ribbon Books, Loveland, Colorado

Belgian Sheepdogs

Copyright © 2003 Marge Turnquist

All rights reserved. No part of this book may be used or reproduced in any manner whatsoever, including electronic media, internet, or newsletters, without written permission from the publisher, except in the case of brief quotations embodied in critical reviews. For permission, write to Alpine Publications, Inc., P. O. Box 7027, Loveland, CO 80537.

Library of Congress Cataloging-in-Publication Data

Turnquist, Marge.
   Belgian sheepdogs / Marge Turnquist.
     p. cm.
   Includes bibliographical references.
   ISBN 1-57779-046-4
    1. Belgian sheepdog. I. Title.

SF429.B4T873 2003
636.737--dc21   2002043992

The information contained in this book is complete and accurate to the best of our knowledge. All recommendations are made without guarantee on the part of the author or Alpine Publications, Inc. The author and publisher disclaim any liability with the use of this information. When Alpine Publications is aware of a trademark claim, we identify the product name by ™ or by using initial capital letters.

This book is available at special quantity discounts for breeders and for club promotions, premiums, or educational use. Write for details.

Design and layout: Laura Newport

Photo Credits:
   Cover and title page: Ch. Rolin Ridge's Fourteen Karat, CD, HC, ROM, CGC, three-time National BISS Winner, bred and owned by Robert and Linda McCarty. Photos by Robert L. McCarty.

   Back Cover : Left, Ch. Sherborne Sterling Sabre, CD, five months of age. Photo courtesy of owner Jill Sherer. Center, Ch. Belle Noire Laxson du Jet, CDX, TT , and right, Ch. GrandFond Duc du Vignoble, UDTX, TT, CGC, HIT, AG, Select, both owned by Kaye Hall and photographed by Donna Golemon of Tandem Dog Sports, Napa, CA.

First printing: February 2003

1 2 3 4 5 6 7 8 9 0

Printed in the United States of America.

Contents

ABOUT THE AUTHOR	iv
INTRODUCTION	vi
CHAPTER 1 — The Story of the Belgian Sheepdog	1
CHAPTER 2 — The Belgian Lifestyle	9
CHAPTER 3 — Choosing the Right Belgian for You	23
CHAPTER 4 — Quality Assurance–The Belgian Standard	31
CHAPTER 5 — For Better or Worse, He's in Your Care	49
CHAPTER 6 — The Well-Behaved Belgian	65
CHAPTER 7 — Off to the Beauty Parlor	73
CHAPTER 8 — In the Limelight	81
CHAPTER 9 — Talent Shows	91
CHAPTER 10 — Herding Work and Competitions	107
CHAPTER 11 — Breeding and Whelping	115
CHAPTER 12 — Pillars in the Breed	127
AFTERWORD	131
APPENDIX A BSCA Awards	133
APPENDIX B Recent BSCA Award Winners	137
Other Sources of Information	143

About the Author

Marge Turnquist is well qualified to write about the Belgian Sheepdog. She is widely known among Belgian Sheepdog owners, having served three times as President of the Belgian Sheepdog Club of America (BSCA), as well as some twenty years as a member of the Club's Board of Directors. At the 1985 National Specialty, she was made a lifetime member of the Club. For more than forty years she has also been a member of the Mid-Continent Kennel Club of Tulsa, and during that time has served in every Club office except President. Her late husband, E. W. (Ed) Turnquist, served as President for that Club where he was well known for his slide lectures on the conformation of dogs. In 1996, Marge was awarded a lifetime membership in the Mid-Continent Kennel Club. She has served on the Board of Directors of two Obedience Clubs in Tulsa as well.

Marge has been an AKC licensed judge of Herding breeds, and has been active for many years in showing dogs in both conformation and obedience, always training and handling her own dogs. She has bred winning Belgian Sheepdogs and German Shepherd Dogs. After she showed her first Belgian puppy to her championship, she bred Ch. Liza del Pirata Nero,CD, to Ch. Zulvo, CD (half brother to Liza's sire, Zordoff). This produced a litter with six champions—just the beginning of the many other champions to follow.

Marge was an instructor of obedience training, and she appeared on a number of television shows featuring conformation as well as obedience training. As a member of the Companion Dog Drill Team, she has participated in demonstrations on training held at schools, veterans' hospitals, and club meetings.

For more than thirty-two years Marge Turnquist authored the Belgian Sheepdog column in the *AKC Gazette*. She also wrote the column for *Dog World*.

Left, Ch. Belle Noire Granada, with breeder/owner Carolyn Hackney; right, author Marge Turnquist with Ch. Belle Noire Torreon.

Introduction

I became interested in Belgian Sheepdogs in 1954 after corresponding with Rudy Robinson and finding out he had an interesting imported litter of Belgian youngsters at his kennel in Muncie, Indiana. I drove up to see them. It was a special litter from a well-known, respected kennel, Pirata Nero in Italy, owned by Angelo Colombo. The pups were sired by Zordoff, Columbo's own special male that was not for sale to anyone. It was a beautiful litter and I found my lovely bitch, Liza, my first Belgian Sheepdog and our foundation bitch for Geier Tal. I joined the BSCA and they put me to work.

The BSCA was a small group and did not have the money to hold a show on their own, so they would pick a large show as centrally located as possible across the country to make it as fair as they could for all the Belgian people to attend. This was the big show of the year; other shows during the year were supported shows.

The Chicago show was a big bench show that lasted three or four days. It was an ideal place to show off a new breed. The dogs had to be on the bench during show hours. We were allowed to decorate our benches. They were decorated very colorfully and the owners stayed with their dogs and were available to answer questions about Belgians. Those days are gone, leaving many happy memories. Now the National Show each year gets bigger and lasts more days. The added activities that our dogs are involved in keep most people busy, and there is little time to relax and visit with each other, but it's fun and the dogs enjoy the attention.

I have been asked my opinion about the old dogs and the dogs today. The majority of old dogs were imports. I didn't get to see all of the old dogs in their prime, but I know that the kennels here and in Europe were trying to breed for a medium-size dog to establish the agility and quickness that were necessary in the breed for herding. The kennels were also trying to establish their own reputations of being reliable for future sales to America.

Most of the older Belgians seemed to be very stable, healthy, and confident that they could take care of any problems. They were not overly friendly, but they did not show fear of people or situations like you see sometimes today. This is where you need a judge to penalize shyness in the ring. That would be a great help in educating people that they need to work with their dogs more. Young dogs may act uncertain at their first shows, but this will pass in most cases if they have love and attention.

Dedicated breeders will try their best to breed as close to the standard as they can. Old Mother Nature sometimes upsets the best-laid plans of man. If you love the breed, you accept this and try to correct your errors and profit by your mistakes.

When a breed gets too popular, you begin to see more poor specimens. If a cute, smart dog is on TV or in a movie, that usually sets off a lot of breeding. When people find out that the cute dog didn't get that way without training, then the fad fades out, but it leaves Rescue Workers with a big problem.

The best advice I can give anyone is to study the bone structure of your dog. Think about what is under the skin and that beautiful hair. Keep in mind the proper bone placement that makes movement effortless and you will add years to your dog's life and your own enjoyment.

Marge Turnquist
Fall 2002

The author, Marge Turnquist, is shown judging Ch. Danny Boy of Ganymede, owner Sheila Rentschler, handler Mike Floyd.

Left: Ch. Johnsondale's Dominique, CDX, HIC (female), owned by Ramona Kraft.
Right: Ch. Johnsondale's Upstart, CD, HIC (male), owned by Shari Kathol.

CHAPTER ONE

The Story of the Belgian Sheepdog

THE BELGIAN SHEEPDOG is a well-balanced, medium-sized black dog, elegant in appearance with a proud carriage of head and neck. He is alert, agile, and full of life. He can run like the wind and stop on a dime. With a quick-witted sense of humor and unusual ingenuity, the Belgian Sheepdog makes an ideal companion for a family of many interests and talents to train and live with.

Belgian Sheepdogs are natural herding dogs, a task for which they were bred many years ago. Their adaptability and intelligence, and proven ability in many areas of work, have made them a popular breed in the twenty-first century.

Belgian Sheepdogs have impressive records in obedience, conformation, search and rescue, Schutzhund trials, tracking, herding, and agility. They have also been quite successful as therapy dogs, guide dogs for the blind, hearing assistance dogs for the deaf, service dogs for the handicapped, and even sled dogs! High on the Belgian Sheepdogs' qualifications, however, have to be their devotion to family, excellence as guardians of the home, and happy dispositions which make them a joy to be around.

Ch. Grand Fond Duc du Vignoble, UDTX, TT, CGC, HIT, AG, Select, is ready to go tracking. Owner, Kaye Hall.

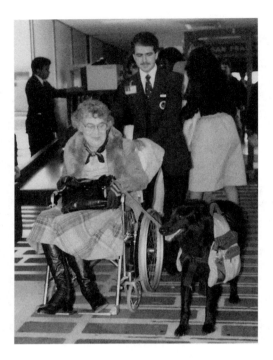

Belgians like to have a job. Here, service dog GrandFond Bonjour is taking her owner Virginia on their first plane ride. Breeder, Kaye Hall.

EARLY BEGINNINGS

The lineage of the Belgian Sheepdog can be traced back to Central Europe, and in particular to the Mooreland dog. The breed was considered the national dog of Belgium and, some believe, inspired Quida's *Dog of Flanders*, and the more famous poet, philosopher, and dramatist Maeterlinck's *Our Friend the Dog*. The original dogs varied in coat—there were longhaired, shorthaired, and rough or wirehaired dogs—but their structure was nearly identical. Eventually a semblance of different types began to develop due to isolation in different localities, and these emerging types were often named for the districts in which they were native.

The history of the Groenendael (longhaired black) Belgian Sheepdog began in 1897. A resident of Uccle, Mr. Bernaerts, had found a Belgian Shepherd dog with long black hair working as a herd dog in Feluy-Arguennes. He was impressed by the beauty, speed, and gentleness the dog displayed while herding the flock. He acquired the dog and named him Piccard D'Uccle. Meanwhile, the proprietor of the Restaurant due Chateau de Groenendael, N. Rose, had already been successful in breeding several Belgian Shepherds with long black hair. He owned a bitch called Petite. She was bred to Mr. Bernaerts' black dog, Piccard D'Uccle, and produced Duc de Groenendael, a fine specimen in every way, with beautiful small ears and good tail carriage, but with a large white marking on his chest. From the same litter came Pitt, Baronne, Margot, and Bergere, all with the suffix "of Groenendael" for the town in which Rose resided. Eventually the kennel name became the name of one of the three types of Belgian Shepherds (the others being the Malinois and the Tervuren).

All of our good Groenendaels (now known as Belgian Sheepdogs) are descendants of these dogs. Piccard D'Uccle was interbred very heavily to his offspring, evidently because the breeders were trying to establish type and coat color.

Groenendaels became quite a vogue. Before World War I, Belgian fanciers were enthusiastic about the black dogs, and at shows there generally were entries of one hundred or more Groenendael specimens. The war curtailed the breeding program enormously. Serious breeders kept some of their best breeding stock, but bred fewer litters. Soon, however, the requests for imports became so great that breeders could not accommodate all of them. Nevertheless, European breeders did not succumb to the lure of money and they continued to produce comparatively few, but consistently fine, Groenendaels.

During World War I, the Groenendaels filled many important posts. They were used on the battlefields in Belgium and France to search for injured soldiers and to convey messages from place to place. The dogs' black coat proved to be perfect camouflage for traveling at night without detection. They were alert companions in the trenches and their faithfulness, obedience, and amiability endeared them to all who depended upon them.

EARLY IMPORTS TO THE UNITED STATES

The exact year that the first imports came to North America is not known. The first Belgians registered by the AKC were imported by Josse Hanssens of Norwalk, Connecticut, in 1911. They were first registered as "German Sheepdogs." There were two Groenendaels, Belgian Dora des Remparts and Belgian Duke, and two listed as auburn—probably of the Malinois type—Ch. Belgian Blackie and Belgian Mouche. In 1912, L. I. de Winter produced the first Groenendael litter in America. Two of the offspring listed were Belgian King Cole (black) and Winterview Dox (black and white).

About 1914, there were six Groenendaels in the kennels of Auguste de Corte, a Belgian immigrant on Staten Island, New York. Harry Weatherby, of Englewood, New Jersey, had purchased Ch. King Cole, and this dog figured conspicuously in the early history of the breed, not only for his show honors, but for his valuable service to the Englewood police. Wetherby and de Corte were active in the promotion of the breed during that era.

During this period there seemed to be a lack of selective breeding, and many mediocre progeny were in evidence. A Mr. M. George Domus of Canada sensed the need for better producers and sent money to Joseph M. Panesi of Antwerp, Belgium, for the procurement of some

Ch. Sherborne InHeirent Charm, bred and owned by Jill Sherer, is a typical twenty-first century Belgian bitch.

good producing Belgians. In 1921, Mr. Domus came into possession of a dog and bitch, Galopin and Netty, the best of their respective strains. The mating of these two was impressive enough to establish the prediction that Mr. Domus would be known as the founder of the Groenendael type on the American continent. Galopin and Netty produced Ch. Jet, Ch. Marco, Ch. Pearl of Belgium, and other progeny. Evidently they were very dominant in their genetic traits, because dogs descended from these two dogs tend to have very similar characteristics.

In a 1917 issue of the magazine *Dogdom*, there was a picture of a Groenendael Sheepdog, Ajax, owned by a Mrs. G. M. Soeter of Brooklyn, New York. This dog was whelped July 28, 1915, in Amsterdam, Holland, and imported by Mrs. Soeter in 1916. This dog was absolutely black and was twenty-six inches in height. He was shown once in Holland and continued to be shown in the United States, winning two firsts, Winners, Best of Breed at one Specialty at

Belgian Sheepdogs are noted for being devoted and intelligent companions. Photo © Kent and Donna Dannen.

Grant City in April, 1917, and two firsts and Winners at the Brooklyn, Long Island Kennel Club Show in May, 1917. Ajax finished his championship quickly. He was so good that he still would be a tough competitor in the ring today.

H. A. Ghislain and his family, natives of Belgium, came to America in 1913. At that time, commercial embargoes prevented importation of dogs, and the laws of Pennsylvania, where Mr. Ghislain became a resident, forbade him, a foreign subject, even to own a dog. It was not until 1921 when Mrs. Ghislain traveled to Belgium on a visit and returned with four Groenendaels—two grown dogs and two puppies—that the family again felt complete with their much-loved Belgian Sheepdogs. They moved to Shreveport, Louisiana. Tragedy struck on the way when one of their adult dogs, a son of Piratin de L'enfer, was killed by a car while exercising by the roadside. The Ghislains reached their destination, and while looking for a country location they rented city property. Unfortunately, they had unfriendly neighbors who disliked dogs, and the neighbors killed the other adult dog. Mr. Ghislain took his case to court, in the vain hope of obtaining redress. He was informed that the law recognized no intrinsic value in the life of a mere dog. Broken-hearted over their loss but undaunted, the Ghislains found some isolated farm land and moved with their remaining two dogs to a safe refuge where they bred and raised many fine Groenendaels that were a credit to the breed. Mr. Ghislain became a naturalized citizen of the United States and a member of the first Belgian Sheepdog Club of America. I have seen pictures of some of the Ghislains' dogs in an old magazine, and I believe those dogs do not look any different from the dogs being shown today, and are perhaps even better.

These were just a few of the pioneers of the breed. Many, many others were important in the breeding programs and in the development of the Belgian Sheepdog in America. Most of their stories will never be told because the information and pictures have been destroyed with the demise of the original Belgian enthusiasts. Each dog in an old pedigree has a poignant story behind his existence, along with the hopes and dreams of his owners and breeders. Some breeders were successful, others dropped out, but all of them contributed something to introducing an unknown breed to the public. It would be interesting to know how these dogs found their way to so many dog shows across the country in the time before there was an organized breed club.

THREE DISTINCT BREEDS

The Belgian Sheepdogs bred in the United States between World Wars I and II were almost all Groenendaels, and thus the longhaired black variety became generally known in the United States as the Belgian Sheepdog.

Training a Belgian for agility helps to give him an outlet for his immense energy and a task to focus his mind on. Handler Cindy Jaye guides Chieho's Zarco Von Jet over a jump.

Their personality makes Belgian Sheepdogs ideally suited for obedience training. Here, a handler returns to her dog after the Stand for Examination exercise. Photo © Judith Strom.

Prior to the 1890s, Belgian sheepdogs were the genuine shepherd's dog, common throughout most of Europe. Belgians today retain this heritage and many excel at herding tests and trials. Photo © Kent and Donna Dannen.

Belgians were widely used as Police Dogs in Europe. The breed is still popular for Schutzhund work and tracking. Here, a handler and dog are working a tracking test. Photo © Judith Strom.

The breed standard describes the Belgian as "elegant in appearance, proud carriage of head and neck. He is a strong, agile, well-muscled animal." And, as shown by this photo, he loves to play. Photo © Christine McHenry.

It was not until the 1940s and '50s that some Malinois, or shorthaired fawn and black dogs, and a number of Tervuren, or longhaired fawn and black Belgians, were imported to America. All three types were registered and shown as Belgian Sheepdogs until July 1, 1959, when the AKC established that they were to become three separate breeds. Belgian Sheepdogs (Groenendaels) were eligible for registration in the United States only if they had at least three generations of pure Groenendael ancestors.

SOME EARLY SHOW RECORDS

Looking back through some old show catalogs of Phyllis Green, a senior member of our local Mid-Continent Kennel Club of Tulsa, Oklahoma, we found that a Belgian Sheepdog was entered in a 1925 show. The dog's name was Commerca. (Breeder, M. M. Bruen. Listed June 25, 1919. Owner, G. Lynn Rohrback.)

In 1925, at Waco, Texas, two Belgians were entered: One was Brussels, by Liege ex Loraine of Belgian. (Breeder, H. H. Johanning, Phoenix, Arizona. Listed September 8, 1924. Owner, V. J. Zienter.) A littermate was entered and offered for sale for $150.00.

In 1927, in Oklahoma City, Oklahoma, there was one Belgian entered in three classes, Puppy Dog, Novice, and Open. This was Rene de Lorrona, by Porthos Deshorrona ex Lady Delenfer. (Breeder, Don Shaffer. Listed March 6, 1927. Owner, Irene Wood.)

In 1932, at the Tulsa Mid-Continent Show, a bitch, Princess Riska, by Fidax ex Charlott, was entered in the Open Class. (Breeder, Mrs. Frank Phillips of Phillips Petroleum in Bartlesville, Oklahoma. Listed October 30, 1930. Owner, George P. Dickson.)

In 1933, at the Tulsa Mid-Continent Kennel Club Show, a dog was entered in the American-Bred Class. This was Philmont Boy, by Sonny Del'Eufer ex Adeline. (Breeder, Waite Phillips. Listed October 22, 1932. Owner, Mrs. J. K. Curran.) This dog went on to Fourth in Group. According to our club Historian, Dave Spang, this probably was the first Belgian Sheepdog to place in Group.

In the '20s and '30s dog shows ran for three days, and most were held in tents. There were few comfortable accommodations available and many people slept in the tents with their dogs. The shows were small, and the exhibitors were like a happy family, roughing it. When you think of the shows today with the big vans, air conditioners, comfortable buildings to show in, and all the modern equipment, you want to take your hat off to the hardy souls who blazed the trail in the depression years.

THE BELGIAN SHEEPDOG CLUB OF AMERICA

The Belgian Sheepdog Club of America was founded in 1925. Officers included Calvin Augustin, president, Margaret Phelan, vice-president, and Edward B. Phelan, secretary-treasurer. Mr. Augustin had written many interesting articles for dog magazines long before this and seemed to have a great knowledge of the breed. He was an active breeder and exhibitor at the time. This club was eventually dissolved, for reasons unknown.

A second parent club was organized in Muncie, Indiana, in 1947. Myron "Ted" Rowland served as president, Rush L. Brown was first vice-president, and Mildred Shepherd was second vice-president.

Ch. Fume Noir, CD, going Best of Breed at the 1951 BSCA National Specialty. He was owned by Rush and Shirley Brown.

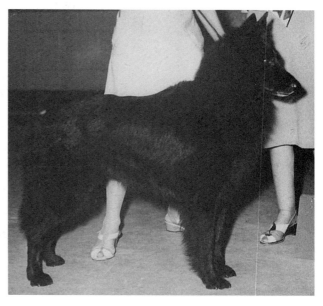

Ch. Lawry Candide, CD, BOB 1962 and 1966 BSCA National Specialties. Owner, Gloria L. Davis. Photo by William Gilbert.

Beatrice Brindel served as secretary-treasurer. A series of sanctioned matches was held soon thereafter to fulfill the requirements for recognition by the American Kennel Club. The club's first application to the AKC was denied due to an inadequate number of members—only thirteen. The club applied to the AKC again in December of 1949 and was finally accepted into membership.

In the minutes of the Board of Directors meeting in March, 1952, a motion was made and carried to list the following charter members in the permanent records of the club: W. B. Vestal, Cecil Lutz, Beatrice Brindel, Arthur Brindel, Rush Brown, Shirley Brown, Rudolf Robinson, Myron Rowland, Mildred L. Shepard, Perry Daily, Marguerite Daily, Ed Hauser, and Mrs. Ed Hauser.

As the club began to grow, other prominent names appeared in the minutes. Among them were Norton, Goris, Mertz, Mills, Orrin Stine, John Cowley, and Margaret Coyle. Many others followed.

The charter club was small but, since the members imported a number of dogs from some of the best kennels in Europe, there was a good genetic pool from which to choose when establishing a breeding program. These original members bred many very good dogs that had great influence on the breed during a time when revitalization was necessary.

The club grew quite rapidly in the 1950s, and membership has continued to increase every year. It now includes around 500 members. Belgian Sheepdogs are taking their rightful place in Group placements and Best in Show awards. It has been a long, rocky road, but this versatile breed is finally being recognized as one of the most proficient dogs in the Herding Group, as well as a great companion dog for people of all ages.

Ch. OTCH U-CD Czequet's Charfire Charon HT, TT, HIC, Am. Sch-H I, WD-X, HOF, CGC, TDI, owned by Elaine Havens, retrieves over the high jump.

CHAPTER TWO

The Belgian Lifestyle

THE PROWESS OF THE BELGIAN Sheepdog in all phases of training and work with humans has not been excelled by any breed. They have proven to be versatile, dependable, and competitive in many different fields of work and recreation.

BELGIAN SHEEPDOGS AT PLAY

Belgian Sheepdogs have a pixieish sense of humor. If you yourself do not have this attribute, then you will not appreciate this trait in Belgians. They are ever alert for any situation that will give them a chance to play pranks on their unsuspecting owners. They also seem enjoy all types of games, and enter into them with enthusiasm and fervor. Belgians love to swim, play in snow, retrieve objects, go jogging with their owners, catch Frisbees, or be involved in any game that requires physical dexterity.

Belgians also adapt well to people who are not as active. They are sensitive to moods and respond with gentle

This Belgian Sheepdog puppy learned to retrieve a ball from the water. Photo © Christine McHenry.

Belgians enjoy family fun, hiking, and camping trips and are ideal companions, as well as guardians, for children.

understanding. They love children and playing children's games, but are also reliable guardians of small children. Their intelligence and adaptability make Belgian Sheepdogs ideal all-around family dogs.

BELGIANS AT WORK

The following is an introduction to some of the many activities you can enjoy with your Belgian. Owning such a talented, enthusiastic, and agile dog will probably eventually draw you into one of the many competitions or activities available. You and your dog will form a stronger bond and become more physically fit and mentally alert because of it. So go for it—read on about just a few of the choices available.

Herding

Belgian Sheepdogs were originally bred as herding dogs and have excelled in this endeavor for many years. A Mr. de Corte, who bred Belgians about 1917, wrote that long before there were railroads between Flanders and Belgium, all the cattle and sheep raised in Flanders had to travel on foot to the Belgian markets. The black Groenendael-type sheepdogs were guardians of the flocks, generally with only one man in charge over the dogs. These dogs were faithful and reliable in their duties and indispensable in moving cattle and sheep across the wild, rough terrain.

Belgian Sheepdogs still retain a natural instinct for herding. They also possess very sensitive hearing and are alert to any noise that could mean harm to their charges. They have speed and a fast takeoff, and are so agile that they can reverse direction to turn back strays without losing ground. Belgians were used to move great flocks of sheep, which always traveled very closely together, and, if frightened by wild animals, were very likely to stampede.

There are unsubstantiated stories of Belgians running across the backs of the sheep and dropping down in front of the flock to stop the panic-stricken animals.

A Belgian has either an even or a scissor bite. The even bite is an asset in herding—sometimes the dog has to nip his charges to get them moving. The scissor bite, on the other hand, will pinch but not tear the skin and is beneficial for holding securely in protection work.

The Belgian Sheepdog was used for herding in Europe for more than a century, but it was not until the latter part of the twentieth century that many people in the United States became aware of the breed's herding ability. Belgian Sheepdogs are used to herd many different animals, including ducks, geese, and turkeys. Sometimes the Belgians' instinct for herding gets them into trouble for herding things that people do not want herded. I know of some young Belgian pups that escaped from their fenced-in yard, went over to a neighboring rancher's spread, rounded up his cattle, put them in the cattle lot, and would not let them out. The charade ended when the dogs' owners were called and the culprits were relieved of their unsolicited efforts at being helpful neighbors.

Belgian fanciers hold herding seminars and compete in various herding tests and trials. City and suburban owners can join in the fun because many clubs purchase and maintain a herd of sheep or lease facilities on the outskirts of metropolitan areas. You don't have to be a farmer to enjoy this popular sport. For more information, refer to the chapter on herding later in this book.

Obedience

Obedience competition is a sport that can be enjoyed by both young and

Belgians excel at working large flocks in open country. Nyjella Ceres Kuymal, RD, HTRD-III-s,d, ATD-d, STD-c, HS, HGH, CGC, owned by Peggy Richter, is gathering sheep in sagebrush-covered pasture.

old. Basic obedience training is essential for all dogs. It makes them better companions and easier to control, and the comradeship that develops between dog and trainer is a very rewarding experience for both. Furthermore, obedience training is the foundation of all the other types of training that have made dogs so valuable in their service to mankind.

At AKC obedience trials, dogs compete at Novice, Open, and Utility levels. They can also go on to earn an Obedience Trial Championship (OTCH). Dogs are scored on a scale of 100 points and must earn a total of eighty-five points out of the hundred to "qualify," plus they cannot fail any of the exercises. Three qualifying scores under at least two different judges entitle a dog to the Companion Dog (CD) title from Novice class, the Companion Dog Excellent (CDX) from the Open class, or the Utility Dog (UD) from the Utility class. Once he has earned a Utility Dog degree, a dog can continue to compete for High in Trial awards or points toward the OTCH.

Belgian Sheepdogs hold more obedience titles per breed registration than the majority of dogs in the Herding and Working Groups. Ch. OTCH Belle Noire Onward Bound is shown here winning HIT at the Belgian Sheepdog National Specialty in Las Vegas. Breeder, Carolyn Hackney; owner/handler, Lance Willig.

Belgians score high in formal obedience competition, and have proven to be tough competitors for "Highest Scoring Dog in Trial" awards. They are willing, happy workers, and their intense desire to please makes them easy to train with minimal effort. They do not respond well to rough treatment or loud voice commands, and therefore do well with the positive reinforcement methods which are popular today. You can learn about obedience competition by joining a dog club, attending puppy or adult obedience classes, or taking private lessons from an obedience trainer. Look in the Yellow Pages under "Dog Training."

Agility

Dog agility is one of the newest events to be offered to the dog fancy, and it is growing in popularity with exhibitors as well as being received enthusiastically from the viewing public. Agility is fun, exciting, and much freer than obedience. Some obedience and conformation competitors find that it loosens their dog up and keeps him excited about going to shows.

Agility made its appearance in Great Britain in 1978 at the Crufts dog show. It was introduced as entertainment for the audience and created so much interest and enjoyment that it rapidly evolved into a competitive event. The sport found its way to the United States around 1985, where it was accepted with great interest from people who enjoyed training their dogs beyond the obedience degree that was available. The United States Dog Agility Association (USDAA) was formed under international rules based on the rules used in Great Britain. Educational programs were set up for judges, instructors, course designs, training techniques, and resolving performance problems. It was a tedious job to iron out all the details before an AKC event could be offered.

Above: Agility is a fast-paced, exciting competition in which the dog and handler race through a course similar to a cross-country jumping course for horses. The run is timed, and the fastest dog to negotiate all the obstacles correctly is declared the winner. Obstacles vary, but usually include: a series of high jumps . . .

Right: an A-frame which the dog must scale, . . .

Below: and a tunnel. Photos © Kent and Donna Dannen.

AKC agility trials give dog owners and trainers a chance to demonstrate their dogs' willingness to work with them under a variety of conditions. A trainer must have good handling skills and be fairly agile in order to direct his or her dog over and through such obstacles as an A-frame, dog walk, seesaw, tunnel, and broad and triple bar jumps. The program begins with entry-level agility, and progresses to higher levels which are more difficult. Dogs that pass the requirements within the time limit gain points toward a degree. Dogs twelve months of age or older that are registered with the AKC are eligible to participate in AKC events. Other organizations also host agility trials. Find out more about them from your local trainer or training academy.

Tracking

Many Belgians love to track, so you and your dog may find this an enjoyable pastime. The dog learns to recognize a person's scent on an object and then follows a track left by that person through a field, finally locating an object placed by the tracklayer. Tracking is a confidence booster for your dog, and it aids in the development of true partnership. The dog is both leader and decision-maker, while you will learn to trust your Belgian's keen sense of smell and to read his body language. Observing his uncanny scenting ability and learning how it works is both fascinating and valuable.

Training a tracking dog means getting up before dawn to lay a track, getting plenty of exercise and conditioning, putting a lot of preparation into your dog's training program, and even traveling a bit to get to the nearest tracking test. It also includes planning, lessons, and keeping written records of the dog's progress and practice tracks.

Tracking tests are administered by the AKC in three different levels. The length, age, and difficulty of the track vary, depending upon the level of test being given. All three tests are non-competitive. Passing the first level will earn the dog the TD (Tracking Dog) title. Passing the second level is much more demanding and earns a TDX (Tracking Dog Excellent). The third and final level, introduced in 1995, the VST (Versatile Surface Tracking), requires following a track laid over various forms of cover such as dirt, concrete, and heavy vegetation. The AKC also awards a CT (Champion Tracker) title to dogs that earn all three other titles.

The handler gives a reward to the dog for finding a glove at the end of a track. Photo © Judith Strom.

SOME BREED RECORDS

First Breed Champion: Either King Cole (Owner, Harry Weatherby) or Ajax (imported from Holland by Mrs. G. M. Soetor). (1920s)

First American and Canadian Champion: Am. Can. Ch. Uhlan Bar Bingen, U.D.T., Can. C.D.X. Owner, Mary Dillaway. (1961)

First American and English Champion: Am. Eng. Ch. Laralee's Traveler. Owner, Doreen Bushby (England). (1971)

First Group Placement: Philmont Boy. Owner, Mrs. J. K. Curran. (1933)

First Group I Placement: Ch. Flicky Candide, C.D. Owner, Dorothea Kelley. (1959)

First Champion Dog Excellent: Ch. Hadji de Flanders, U.D.T. Owner, Clara Vestal. (1940s)

First Champion Dog Excellent (Bitch): Dianne de Beaute Noir, C.D.X. Owner, Art Brindel. (1949)

First Utility Dog: Ch. Hadji De Flanders, U.D.T. Owner, Clara Vestal. (1947)

First Utility Dog (Bitch): Sheba III de Beaute Noir, U.D. Owner, Rudy Robinson. (1950)

First Utility Dog Tracking: Ch. Hadji de Flanders, U.D.T. Owner, Clara Vestal. (1948)

First Utility Dog Tracking (Bitch): Ch. A'Dew Skipon Rebel O'Ebon Will, U.D.T. Owner, Stephanie Jay Price. (1981)

First Champion Dog Tracking (Bitch): Vicki Carobingen, C.D., T.D. Owner, Rita Catsby. (1963)

First Obedience Trial Champion: Windstorm V. Siegestor, T.D., P.C., E.T., A.T.D., INT. Sch-H III Ch. Owner-Breeder, Kurt Marti. (1979)

First Schutzhund I Champion: Mex. Am. Ch. Bruce V. Kaiserhof, Sch-H III. Owner, Kurt Marti. (1970)

First Schutzhund I Champion (Bitch): Ch. Laralee's Personality, C.D., Sch-H I. Owner, Pat Crabtree. (1974)

First Schutzhund II Champion: Ch. Fireball V. Siegestor, U.D., Sch-H III. Owner, Elaine Hornbuckle. (1971)

First Schutzhund III Champion: Mex. Am. Ch. Bruce V. Kaiserhof, Sch-H III. Owner, Kurt Marti (1972)

First AD: Am. and Mex. Ch. Rafer V. Siegestor, U.D., Sch-H I, A.D. Owner, Elaine Hornbuckle. (1972)

First Triple Champion Bitch: Mex. Am., and Can. Ch. Johnsondale's High-Mount Indigo. Owner, Pat Johnson. (1978)

First Group Winner: Ch. Dianne De Beaute Noir, C.D.X. Owner, Mr. and Mrs. Arthur Brindel. (Late 1940s)

First Best in Show Winner: Am. Can. Ch. Skip's Reward O'Ebon Will. Owner, Mrs. William Hendricks. (1973)

First E.T. (or A.D.): Mex. Am. Ch. Rafer V. Siegestor, U.D., Sch-H I, A.D. Owner, Elaine Hornbuckle (1972)

First Master Agility Champion (MACH) and First U.S. Flyball Grand Champion: Ch. MACH2 Shalyn Dances on Heir. Owners, Kurt and Jean Matushek. (2001)

Top Left: The first Obedience Trial Champion of the breed, Mex. Am. Ch. OTCh. Windstorm V. Siegestor, TD, PC, ET, ATD, Int. Sch-H III Ch. Breeder and owner, Kurt Marti.

Above Right: First Companion Dog Excellent, Utility Dog, and Utility Dog Tracking, Ch. Hadji de Flanders, U.D.T., with owner Clara Vestal.

Left: The first Best in Show winner, also BOB at the 1972 and '73 BSCA National Specialties. Am. Can. Ch. Skip's Reward O'Ebon Will was owned by Mrs. William Hendricks.

Schutzhund

Schutzhund is an extension of obedience training which includes protection training and attack work. A dog that has won his degrees in an official Schutzhund trial is a well-trained animal that will do equally well in the obedience ring, in tracking or search and rescue, or in the defense of his owner, family, and home. Some people participate in Schutzhund for the challenge; others choose the training because of the protection aspect. In order to reach his full potential, the working dog must have a sound, stable temperament. Overly aggressive or shy dogs should not be used.

While Schutzhund training and trials are comparatively new to the United States, they have been popular in Europe for centuries. Due perhaps to a rise in crime, the sport has become more popular in the United States in recent years. The first Schutzhund trial in the United States was held in 1969-1970, and Belgian Sheepdogs placed first and second in the competition.

There are a number of Schutzhund clubs in the United States, but they do not offer their training to the general public as do the obedience clubs. Schutzhund clubs are for members only.

The Schutzhund I, II, and III degrees, recognized worldwide, each consist of three parts:

A) Tracking
B) Obedience
C) Protection

Each of the three sections is scored on a scale of 100 points, for a possible total score of 300. In order to pass the test, the dog must score at least 70 points in the A and B sections and at least 80 points in the C section. The dog must earn the Schutzhund I degree before proceeding to Schutzhund II competition. As each successive degree is earned, the previous degree is dropped and the new degree added behind the dog's name.

The rules governing Schutzhund trials are set forth by the North American Working Dog Association (NASA), an independent, non-profit organization established under the rules of the World Dog Federation (Federation Cynologique Internationale, or FCI), with headquarters in Belgium. NASA maintains that a dog is only as beautiful as he is functional. To perform properly, the dog must be both mentally and anatomically correct.

Schutzhund training is not for every person or every dog. It is an advanced level of training, so you should try Obedience and Tracking training first; then if you are interested in the protection aspect as well, find a good Schutzhund club and attend some trials and lessons to decide if you have the dedication, time, and stamina to devote to this intense discipline. The instructor will also help you evaluate your dog's temperament and physical suitability for the sport.

Search and Rescue

Search and rescue training covers many phases of humanitarian endeavor.

Mex. Am. Ch. OTCH Windstorm V. Siegestor, TD, PC, ET, ATD, Int. Sch-H III Ch., owned by Kurt Marti, is pictured in Schutzhund training. The dog must learn to attack, and also to stop his aggression on the command of his handler.

Dogs are trained to rescue victims of earthquakes, tornadoes, and avalanches, and to find persons lost in rural or wilderness areas. We all have read in newspapers of dogs being used to search in rubble and debris for victims of a disaster. The dogs' keen hearing and sense of smell can direct them to victims who would be overlooked by human searchers. Many lives have been saved by courageous trainers and their search and rescue dogs.

Much of the training is based on an extension of obedience exercises. The trainer has to have complete control of his dog at all times. The obedience exercises used for this work are on-leash and off-leash heeling, the direct-go or send-out exercise, scent discrimination, and the long down-stay with the handler out of sight. Search and rescue dogs learn to crawl through openings, to proceed with caution, and to be alert to unstable debris and terrain. When a victim is located, the dog alerts his handler and stays in place until help arrives.

The average working life span of a rescue dog is eight years. It takes months of training to qualify for search and rescue work. Since adult dogs have but a few years to work after completion of their training, advocates of this type of work sometimes start training future search and rescue dogs as young as eight weeks.

The training is begun in easy stages, with plenty of socialization with people and other dogs, riding in cars, and being exposed to new situations and places that will give the dogs confidence and help them adapt to change and noise which they will encounter in later training. Basic obedience can be introduced at this point, with the dog learning to walk on lead, to sit on command, and to come when called. This training requires patience, and lots of praise when the dog responds. Tracking can be fun for the puppy as he learns to use his nose to find his handler, concealed a short distance away. The reward should be lots of praise and a good romp together. The distance should be increased gradually, and other members of the family can be included in this game.

Learning to walk across unstable boards is another part of training, and is often frightening to a puppy. The handler should never push the puppy, but should give him voice encouragement and pet him when he takes some steps forward. When he makes it across, the praise should be lavish, with plenty of petting. If the puppy gets lots of attention, he will be willing to try again. Soon he will get his "sea legs," and another obstacle will have been surmounted. A puppy is naturally curious, which makes learning and adapting to new situations much easier for him than for an adult dog.

Search and rescue teams that are ready to help in any emergency have been organized throughout America. These teams became very important to people in Oklahoma when the tragic bombing of the Federal Building in Oklahoma City took place on April 19, 1995, and again during the devastation at the World Trade Center in New York in 2001. Trainers and their dogs did not wait to be asked—they were ready and on their way. They worked hours and days in dangerous conditions to locate victims and bodies. The dogs had to wear boots on their feet to protect them from broken glass and twisted steel. Belgian Sheepdogs and other breeds working together in teams were beautiful to watch. The dogs were not in show trim; they were tired and disheveled, but their dedication to their job made each one an outstanding specimen of their breed.

"Choucas," GrandFond Cyclone TT, a ski patrol and avalanche rescue dog, is going out with his handler to find a "victim." Breeder, Kaye Hall.

He has almost reached the place where his victim has been buried under eight feet of snow.

Choucas has successfully located and dug down to the victim.

If you aspire to this kind of community service, you and your dog both must maintain excellent physical condition, and you must be available on a moment's notice—day or night, ready to travel wherever you may be called. Search and rescue teams work all over North and South America and sometimes travel to other continents as well. You must be able to endure hardship, lack of sleep and food, and bad weather during the search. You will know the disappointment of finding victims too late, as well as the elation that comes when a life is saved. The reward for your labor is knowing that, as a team, you perform a service to humanity that no human being can do alone.

Avalanche Rescue

Avalanche dogs were first developed in Austria, and the first dogs to be used for this work were Belgian Sheepdogs. In avalanche rescue, the dog has to search in ice and snow. When he finds a victim he will start to dig. His sense of smell is so keen that he can detect a body covered with several feet of snow and debris. The handler and the dog must be in good physical condition and have a close working relationship. The dog must also have a stable, sound temperament to go through the rigorous training necessary for this work.

Rob Greger of Bozeman, Montana, with his racing sled team of Belgians.

Mr. Leo Light with a team of five Belgians at a sled dog derby in Winnepeg, Manitoba. Mattern photo.

Search and rescue work is the most physically and mentally demanding of all the services rendered by a handler and his dog. Catastrophes do not happen at a convenient time or place. Rescue teams may be called to go by helicopter to mountainous areas that cannot be reached by foot. The rescuers have to be ready to go by any conveyance available, often under severe climatic conditions, and work for hours or days at a stretch to accomplish their mission. They are unsung heroes, unpaid volunteers who subject themselves and their dogs to numerous hardships. Their only reward is in finding a missing person who might have perished without their help, and in the gratitude of the families and friends of the victims.

Sheba III de Beauté Noir, UD, and Ch. Dulci Candide, CD, owned by Rudy Robinson, pull a cart.

Dog Sledding

Belgians are currently entering another field—sledding—which should prove most interesting. Belgian sled dog teams are making their debut in the racing circles. Their speed and lightness of foot should serve as great assets to their success in this sport. In Alaska, Belgians are recognized for speed and the ability to adapt to extreme weather conditions because of their all-weather coat. Pulling a sled should not be too foreign to Belgians; they once pulled milk carts in

GrandFond Bonjour was the first Belgian Sheepdog and the youngest dog ever to graduate from CCI. Here she accompanies her owner Virginia on their first plane ride.

Bonjour and Virginia go to the bank.

"Breeze" graduates as a service dog for Canine Companions for Independence. Breeder, Kaye Hall.

their native country. A few Belgian owners have taught their dogs to pull carts or skijour (pull people on skis). I would not be surprised to see more of these activities in the future as well.

Service Dogs

This is not an activity that normal owners and dogs perform together. However, as an owner, you may need a service dog, or as a breeder you may have an opportunity to donate a puppy for this type of work. Assistance dogs are trained by organizations such as Canine Companions for Independence (CCI), and matched with individuals as service, hearing, skilled companion, and facility dogs. A service dog helps a person with a physical disability, performing practical tasks to assist the owner, such as carrying or picking up objects, pressing elevator buttons or turning on lights.

A Hearing Dog is trained to alert the owner to sounds, including telephones,

GrandFond Chelsea of CCI is a signal dog for her deaf couple, Paul and Anne Ogden. Breeder, Kaye Hall.

alarm clocks, and smoke alarms. A Skilled Companion Dog is placed with adults or children to facilitate social, interactive, and motion skills. A Facility Dog works with a professional caregiver to help provide physical, emotional, or developmental care to those physically or emotionally challenged individuals or to the elderly.

Therapy Dogs

You can gain great satisfaction from joining groups of people who use their dogs to visit senior citizen retirement centers. Most of the people that are confined for various reasons have owned a special dog in their lifetime, and seeing and being able to caress a well-behaved dog brings back happy memories. They like to tell stories about their beloved old dogs, and the joy you see on their faces will be a rewarding experience because you know your dog made someone's day a little happier. Dogs are an important part of our lives for service, protection and love. Where else could you get so much for so little?

Children usually enjoy Belgian puppies. Star Wolf's Gangster with Pedro Ferraro. Owner/breeder, Juan Carlos Ferraro, Buenos Aires, Argentina.

CHAPTER THREE

Choosing the Right Belgian for You

THE SELECTION OF A PUPPY of any breed to become a member of your household should be approached with caution and much consideration. All puppies are adorable when they are small—especially Belgians, which look like little black teddy bears—but they grow up fast. Belgians need plenty of exercise to develop properly and to run off excess energy.

Take your time and find a Belgian Sheepdog breeder who has a reputation for being reliable and for dealing honestly with a prospective client. You can find the name and address of the secretary of the Belgian Sheepdog Club of America in the *AKC Gazette*, or you can check out the American Kennel Club website for the information. The secretary may be able to direct you to breeders within driving distance of your home.

Make an appointment to see the puppies and their dam, and the sire if possible. Their behavior will give you an idea of what you can expect when one of their puppies becomes an adult. If either the sire or dam is shy, backing

---

THINGS TO CONSIDER

- Have you researched the breed and visited breeders so that you are sure this is the right breed for you?
- Do you know what you want to do with your dog when he is grown? Will you show him or enter any kind of competition? What kind of training do you plan to do?
- Do you want a family dog or a "one-person" dog?
- Do you plan to breed your dog at some point? If so, you will want to choose a worthy specimen.
- If you are purchasing a companion dog, are you willing to have him neutered or spayed?
- Do you have ample space for a Belgian to exercise—either a fairly large yard or exercise pen?
- Do you have time to give the dog the attention and discipline during the formative months that will make him a well-mannered, affectionate, devoted companion?

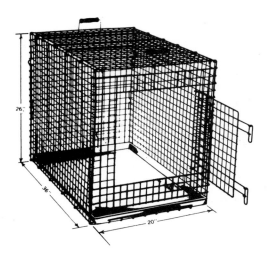

A wire crate suitable in size for an adult Belgian Sheepdog.

Which puppy will it be? Eight-week-old puppies out of Ch. Lorjen Marjorie Morningstar bred by Roger and Maxine Ellis.

away with tail tucked between legs while barking continually, you should visit another kennel. This is not a dog with sound temperament, and whether it is a learned or inherited behavior, the chances are high that some of the puppies will behave in the same manner.

When you do find a puppy, it will be much easier to bring him home with you and not risk the trauma of shipment by air. Take a dog crate with you to confine the puppy on the way home. A wire crate allows plenty of air circulation and the puppy will travel better if he can see people. This will make him feel that he is not alone and will give him confidence to deal with the new experience of riding in a car. Line the crate with plenty of newspapers.

Ask the breeder to bring out only those specimens that are for sale and are of the sex you are interested in. Trying to view an entire litter of puppies at once can be confusing. Some puppies will be cautious with strangers until they sense that all is well. It is best to get down on the puppy's level, either sitting or squatting. A strange person standing up can look pretty formidable to a young puppy. Never force yourself on a puppy, but let him come to you.

The health of the puppy is the first consideration. All the puppies should look well cared for, full of life, playful, and friendly. The coat should be clean and free of parasites, and the eyes should be clear and alert, with no signs of discharge.

In my opinion, the best way to select puppies is to get down on their level rather than looking down at them. Then watch for good side movement, as well as movement going and coming. Look for alertness and an outgoing personality. Watch the puppies move about freely. Usually there is one that will catch your eye. Sometimes a puppy will choose you, and that will be a good choice, assuming he has the other qualities for which you are looking.

If you are picking a dog for a companion only, the choice is simpler. All you have to be concerned about is health and temperament. Make sure that the puppy is at least eight weeks old.

This lovely puppy turned out to be Ch. Searcher de Loup Noir, owned by Laura Patton.

If you want a performance prospect, look for the puppy that is responsive, playful, and will come when called or follow you around. You may want to have a trainer go with you to temperament test the puppies. Don't buy the shy, clinging-vine puppy for performance. Choose a puppy with self-confidence and an outgoing personality, but one that is not too independent. If you are choosing a future herding dog, the more independent puppy may be a good choice, assuming that he comes from parents that have proven herding ability. The best performance prospects are bred for the sport or event. One or both parents should have been trained and excelled in that event.

If you want a show prospect, the choice becomes more involved. You want the puppy with the best structure and outline that you can obtain, plus you need a bold, confident puppy with a "look at me" personality. It is wiser to choose an older puppy, because even an expert cannot accurately predict what a small puppy will look like when it matures. Characteristics which suggest show quality include substantial bone, good temperament, outgoing personality, sound body, compact feet, good coat, good teeth and correct bite. Most breeders will be glad to point out the differences among puppies and advise you which puppies have show quality potential. Your best chance of getting a possible show quality puppy is to buy from a breeder whose lines have produced champions, and who has been successful in show competition.

BEFORE YOU BRING YOUR PUPPY HOME

Following is a list of items that you will want to have on hand before you pick up your new puppy:

- A nylon buckle collar about 12 inches long
- Two non-spill 16 ounce bowls for food and water
- A six-foot nylon lead
- A tennis ball or a rubber ball about the same size
- Chewable items like rawhides, pig ears, or a dental rope
- A medium-size stuffed toy
- Dog food of the same variety the breeder is feeding
- A nail clipper and brush for grooming
- A good brand of carpet cleaner/deodorizer
- A crate or pen for your puppy.

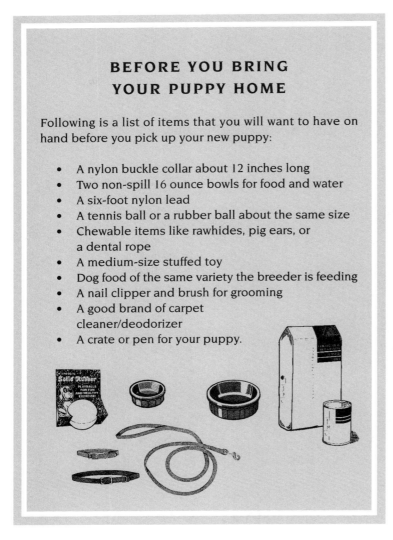

REGISTRATION AND PAPERS

When you buy a purebred dog from anyone, regardless of that person's reputation, have all the terms of the agreement in writing before you leave with a puppy. Many breeders agree to let the puppy be checked by the purchaser's own veterinarian. If there is a problem, the purchaser can return the dog and the breeder will provide a replacement, if available, or return the purchaser's money. Whatever agreement you work out *must* be in writing. Otherwise, if the breeder does not live up to the agreement, you do not have written proof should you need to take civil action or make a protest to the AKC.

The breeder should provide you with the puppy's inoculation and worming records, a schedule for feeding, and information as to the type of food provided for the puppy. (An abrupt change in food can cause diarrhea.) The breeder should provide at least a three-generation pedigree and either an AKC registration certificate or an application form. Some breeders name and register each puppy individually. If this has been done, you will have to complete the transfer and send the form, with fee, to the AKC. They will transfer the dog to your name and send you a new certificate. If you receive an application for registration, you should fill it out, choosing a name for your dog, and mail it to the American Kennel Club immediately with the correct fee (which is listed on the application).

FIRST NIGHT IN THE NEW HOME

The first night in a new home can be traumatic for both the puppy and the new owner. This will probably be the first night the puppy has spent away from his littermates, with whom he once cuddled up to sleep. He may be confused and frightened.

Let the crate in which he was brought home become his refuge. Cover the back half of the crate to create a dark place for him to rest. Line the crate with layers of paper. A loud-ticking alarm clock placed beside the crate will be a comforting sound, reminiscent of the heartbeat of his siblings, and a radio playing soft music will make the puppy feel he is not completely alone. Give him a large Milkbone to chew on in case he gets hungry, but it is best to withhold water during the night to aid with housebreaking. A safe stuffed puppy toy is also comforting. In just a few nights your new puppy should adjust.

HEALTH CHECK

Take your puppy to visit your veterinarian as soon as possible. Bring along a stool specimen for a worm check, and the worming and inoculation records provided by the breeder so that your veterinarian can continue the pup's original schedule. Be sure to ask your veterinarian about heartworm medication, rabies shots, licensing, and other preventive inoculations which the puppy will need. Take your veterinarian's advice and keep on schedule with the suggested program. If the veterinarian detects a serious health problem in the puppy, however, you must notify the breeder immediately in order to get a replacement or any adjustment of the purchase price.

FEEDING AND CARE

The breeder should give you a few days' supply of the food the puppy is currently eating and tell you how much to feed him. Most puppies do best on a high quality dry food formulated for puppies that is moistened with warm water and fed three times a day. When the pup reaches six months of age, feeding him twice a day is sufficient. Feed your puppy on a regular time schedule, and do not overfeed. Overly fat puppies are more prone to developing hip dysplasia or joint problems. Puppies that overeat are more likely to have diarrhea or loose stools and be difficult to housebreak.

Clean, fresh water should be available at all times during the day, but limit

A stuffed toy often comforts a new puppy. Be sure that any button eyes or nose that the puppy could tear off and swallow are safely removed.

water at night until the puppy's bladder is mature enough to allow him to get through the night without urinating.

Never allow a young puppy to have freedom in the house without constant supervision. Everything goes into a puppy's mouth. Certain houseplants are poisonous. Cleaners and poisonous chemicals (under the sink in most kitchens) can be lethal. Electrical outlet cords should always be disconnected or out of reach. Puppy teeth are sharp and can penetrate a cord easily, causing severe shock or death. If you are in the room and the puppy starts to chew on something he shouldn't, pick up a magazine or fly swatter, and while the puppy is not looking, either throw the magazine near him or bang the fly swatter on something to make a sharp noise as you give the command "NO!" If this is done so that it startles the dog, he will associate something unpleasant with chewing. If the damage has been done while you were not present, do not punish the puppy. His memory is short, and he has probably forgotten what he did. If he left

Where did that squirrel go? Belgian puppies are very curious and like to check things out. Breeder, Pat Snow.

a puddle on the floor or a pile of chewed-up papers, it is all right to take him to the spot and ask in a firm tone of voice, "Did you do that? Bad dog!" Punishment depends on the dog's temperament. Some dogs learn from one bad experience, while others are more willful and have to be corrected repeatedly before they are convinced.

Your puppy will not get all of his adult teeth until he is about eight months of age. Until that time he will be "teething," and just like a human baby, will need items that he can chew to alleviate the pain and help the teeth come in. Rubber or rawhide chew toys are popular. A piece of knotted rope, a tennis ball, dog bones, and stuffed toys made for dogs will be needed. This is the ideal time to teach your dog to retrieve a toy, fetch a designated item, or put his toys away in a box. Toys are great motivators if you don't overuse them. Call the puppy to you and reward him with a short play period with his favorite toy. Play a game of chase or retrieve, followed by a rest period during which you ask the puppy to lie down and stay. Then, as a reward, play another game with a favorite toy. If you take advantage of the puppy's eagerness and enthusiasm during his first four months of life to shape the desired behavior, he will remember it for a lifetime.

Puppies must be taught not to snatch food out of your hand or off the table. Give food rewards some of the time during training sessions, but be sure the puppy takes it gently and politely. Holding a treat directly over the puppy's nose and then slowly moving it backward, just out of his reach, will compel most dogs to sit. Give the command, Sit, simultaneously and reward the puppy with the treat as soon as he has both haunches on the floor. Treats also make a good reward when teaching the puppy to come, or when you first start him walking beside you on a leash. Alternate treats and praise as training progresses, until you are giving more verbal praise and fewer food rewards.

All breeds of puppies are going to run, bark, and dig to some extent, and depending on their temperament, some puppies will do so more than others. A puppy play area will keep your puppy from being bored and prevent many problems. The area might include obstacles to go over and under, toys, and balls. If a puppy is digging, try partially filling the hole, cover the hole with chicken wire, and then finish filling with dirt. This will prevent the pup from digging in a "favorite spot."

HOUSE TRAINING

Housebreaking is best accomplished by feeding the puppy at the same time every day, taking him out within a few minutes after eating, as soon as he awakes in the morning, and immediately

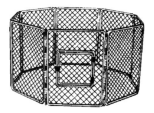

An exercise pen is a helpful item to have when house training a new puppy.

Belgian puppies usually enjoy children. Verseau's Forever George, bred by Ramona Kraft.

after he awakens from a nap. Soon, you will notice him becoming restless or going to the door. Take him out quickly, to the same spot in the yard each time, and reward him for doing his business. When you can't be with the puppy to observe and to let him out when he needs to go, keep him confined to a small pen or area covered with newspaper. Numerous types of puppy pens can be purchased at your local pet store, or you can make your own with 4 x 4 foot panels small mesh wire attached to a 1 x 2 inch frame. Shape the panels into a square and either lock or bungee the corners together so that the panels form a four-foot square pen.

Preventing "accidents" by confining your puppy is much better than allowing them to happen and then trying to correct the problem behavior. Most puppies, if kept on this strict routine, will be dependably housebroken by the time they are three or four months old. It is unrealistic to expect them to have total bowel and bladder control before that age.

BELGIANS AND CHILDREN

Dogs and children are a natural combination: They think alike, they act alike, and they train alike. Both have an abundance of energy that must be channeled in the right direction. Children should be taught to respect the rights of a puppy, just as they respect the rights of their playmates. They should not be allowed to maul a puppy or play until the puppy is exhausted. If children and dogs are taught to play safely together, it can be the most enjoyable time of their lives.

Even the best-natured puppy will finally lose his temper if agitated persistently. Never lift up a puppy by his legs. The bones and ligaments have not matured and severe damage can occur.

The puppy will need rest periods and a place to which he can escape and rest undisturbed. Never let a child pounce on a sleeping dog. The dog may be startled and, since his first instinct is to protect himself, he may bite. Children should not be allowed to play tug-of-war (pull against something the dog is holding in his mouth) with a young puppy. This could pull the dog's mouth out of shape or cause damage to his teeth. It also teaches the dog the power of his teeth and may lead to serious biting or to pulling on anything that offers resistance.

Ch. Rolin Ridge's Fourteen Karat, CD, HIC, ROM, CGC, bred and owned by Robert and Linda McCarty, is a classic example of the male Belgian Sheepdog.

Chapter Four
Quality Assurance – The Belgian Standard

THE BREED STANDARD established by the national breed club serves as a guide for people to use in evaluating their dogs. It presents a picture image or description of the ideal Belgian Sheepdog. Every owner, and especially every breeder or exhibitor, should read and study the breed Standard to learn the desired qualities of his breed. However, it is impossible to know and understand the qualities of an outstanding specimen just by reading the Standard. It takes time, experience, the observation of many dogs, and the study of dogs in general to know what makes a champion.

The first thing to remember is that a dog is a complete unit. Each part of the dog's structure has a bearing on the function of another part or several parts. When one part is not capable of completing its function in this complicated assembly of bones and muscles, that part will be stressed. Nature will try to compensate by building up the muscles, with the result that the dog will become unbalanced. A dog that is structurally unbalanced cannot function correctly, nor will he have the stamina of a dog that is correctly put together.

GENERAL APPEARANCE

The Belgian Sheepdog should have solidity without bulkiness. Since the breed is well known for its agility and for being able to make quick turns (which are necessary in herding), the breeding of larger dogs would defeat the purpose for which the breed was intended. The breeding of small specimens that have fragile bone structure and no substance should also be discouraged. Any extreme deviation from medium size is a fault.

PERSONALITY

The Belgian Sheepdog should be endowed with the qualities of intelligence, courage, and alertness that are necessary for the purpose for which the breed is intended. Originally, Belgian Sheepdogs were bred to guard flocks of sheep, as well as to protect their homes and families.

A dog is influenced by inherited traits as well as by his environment. Good breeding and reliable ancestors are essential. If the ancestors shown in your dog's pedigree are unstable, then there is a

THE AMERICAN KENNEL CLUB STANDARD FOR THE BELGIAN SHEEPDOG

General Appearance
The first impression of the Belgian Sheepdog is that of a well-balanced, square dog, elegant in appearance, with an exceedingly proud carriage of the head and neck. He is a strong, agile, well-muscled animal, alert and full of life. His whole conformation gives the impression of depth and solidity without bulkiness. The male dog is usually somewhat more impressive and grand than his female counterpart. The bitch should have a distinctly feminine look.

Faults
Any deviation from these specifications is a fault. In determining whether a fault is minor, serious, or major, these two factors should be used as a guide: 1. The extent to which it deviates from the standard. 2. The extent to which such deviation would actually affect the working ability of the dog.

Size, Proportion, Substance
Males should be 24-26 inches in height and females 22-24 inches, measured at the withers.
Males under 22 1/2 or over 27 1/2 inches in height and females under 20 1/2 or over 25 1/2 inches in height shall be disqualified.
The length, measured from point of breastbone to point of rump, should equal the height. Bitches may be slightly longer. Bone structure should be moderately heavy in proportion to his height so that he is well balanced throughout and neither spindly or leggy nor cumbersome and bulky. The Belgian Sheepdog should stand squarely on all fours. **Side view** The topline, front legs, and back legs should closely approximate a square.

Head
Clean-cut and strong, overall size should be in proportion to the body.
Expression indicates alertness, attention, readiness for activity. Gaze should be intelligent and questioning. **Eyes** brown, preferably dark brown. Medium size, slightly almond shaped, not protruding. **Ears** triangular in shape, stiff, erect, and in proportion to the head in size. Base of the ear should not come below the center of the eye. Ears hanging (as on a hound) shall disqualify.

Skull
Top flattened rather than rounded. The width approximately the same, but not wider than the length. **Stop** moderate. **Muzzle** moderately pointed, avoiding any tendency to snipiness, and approximately equal in length to that of the topskull. The jaws should be strong and powerful. **Nose** black without spots or discolored areas. The lips should be tight and black, with no pink showing on the outside.

Teeth
A full complement of strong, white teeth, evenly set. Should not be overshot or undershot. Should have either an even bite or a scissors bite.

Neck, Topline, Body
Neck round and rather outstretched, tapered from head to body, well muscled, with tight skin. **Topline**–The withers are slightly higher and slope into the back, which must be level, straight, and firm from withers to hip joints. **Chest** not broad, but deep. The lowest point should reach the elbow, forming a smooth ascendant curve to the abdomen. **Abdomen**–Moderate development. Neither tucked up nor paunchy. The *loin* section, viewed from above, is relatively short, broad and strong, but blending smoothly into the back. The *croup* is medium long, sloping gradually. **Tail** strong at the base, bone to reach hock. At rest the dog holds it low, the tip bent back level with the hock. When in action he raises it and gives it a curl, which is strongest toward the tip, without forming a hook. Cropped or stump tail shall disqualify.

Forequarters
Shoulder long and oblique, laid flat against the body, forming a sharp angle (approximately 90 degrees) with the upper arm. **Legs** straight, strong and parallel to each other. Bone oval rather than round. Development (length and substance) should be well proportioned to the size of the dog. Pastern medium length, strong, and very slightly sloped. **Feet** round (cat footed), toes curved close together, well padded. Nails strong and black, except that they may be white to match white toe tips.

Hindquarters

Legs—Length and substance well proportioned to the size of the dog. Bone oval rather than round. Legs are parallel to each other. **Thighs** broad and heavily muscled. The upper and lower thigh bones approximately parallel the shoulder blade and upper arm respectively, forming a relatively sharp angle at stifle joint. The angle at the hock is relatively sharp, although the Belgian Sheepdog does not have extreme angulation. Metatarsus medium length, strong and slightly sloped. Dewclaws, if any, should be removed. **Feet** slightly elongated. Toes curved close together, well padded. Nails strong and black, except that they may be white to match white toe tips.

Coat

The guard hairs of the coat must be long, well fitting, straight and abundant. They should not be silky or wiry. The texture should be a medium harshness. The undercoat should be extremely dense, commensurate, however, with climatic conditions. The Belgian Sheepdog is particularly adaptable to extremes of temperature or climate. The hair is shorter on the head, outside of the ears, and lower part of the legs. The opening of the ear is protected by tufts of hair.
Ornamentation—Especially long and abundant hair, like a collarette, around the neck; fringe of long hair down the back of the forearm; especially long and abundant hair trimming the hindquarters, the breeches; long, heavy and abundant hair on the tail.

Color

Black. May be completely black, or may be black with white, limited as follows: Small to moderate patch or strip on forechest. Between pads of feet. On *tips* of hind toes. On chin and muzzle (frost may be white or gray). On *tips* of front toes—allowable, but a fault.

Disqualification

Any color other than black, except for white in specified areas. Reddening due to climatic conditions in an otherwise correct coat should not be grounds for disqualification.

Gait

Motion should be smooth, free and easy, seemingly never tiring, exhibiting facility of movement rather than a hard driving action. He tends to single track on a fast gait; the legs, both front and rear, converging toward the center line of gravity of the dog. The backline should remain firm and level, parallel to the line of motion, with no crabbing. He shows a marked tendency to move in a circle rather than a straight line.

Temperament

The Belgian Sheepdog should reflect the qualities of intelligence, courage, alertness and devotion to master. To his inherent aptitude as a guardian of flocks should be added protectiveness of the person and property of his master. He should be watchful, attentive, and always in motion when not under command. In his relationship with humans, he should be observant and vigilant with strangers, but not apprehensive. He should not show fear or shyness. He should not show viciousness by unwarranted or unprovoked attack. With those he knows well, he is most affectionate and friendly, zealous of their attention, and very possessive. Viciousness is a disqualification.

Disqualifications

Males under 22 1/2 or over 27 1/2 inches in height and females under 20 1/2 or over 25 1/2 inches in height.
Ears hanging (as on a hound).
Cropped or stump tail.
Any color other than black.
Viciousness.

Approved December 11, 1990
Effective January 30, 1991

Ch. Liza del Pirata Nero, CD, BOS at the 1956 BSCA National, remains a typical example of a show quality Belgian Sheepdog bitch. Owners, Marge and Ed Turnquist.

Head study of BIS Ch. Rolin Ridge's Fourteen Karat, CD, HIC, ROM, CGC.

HEAD

The head is the first thing you notice and remember about a dog. The size of the head, the expression, and the set of the ears should blend to form a pleasing picture. The head also can give you insight into the temperament and personality of the dog. However, good head qualities are of far more importance than mere beauty, for muscles in the head, even though unseen, also affect the gait.

The skull should be flattened rather than round. The width is approximately equal to, but not greater than, the length. The stop should be moderate. The muzzle is moderately pointed, with no tendency to snipiness, and approximately equal in length to the backskull.

The ears should be proportional in size to the head and body. They should be triangular in shape, stiff, and erect. The base of the ear should not come below the center of the eye. Belgians are noted for their small ears, and long ears can create problems. Sometimes the texture of the ear is too thin and soft to support the weight and the ears will fail to become erect. This usually is an inherited trait. Weak head muscles, improper ear set, or injured cartilage can also contribute to this problem.

The ears are a dog's greatest asset. The human ear can hear sounds ranging between 1,500 and 15,000 vibrations per second. The dog can hear sounds that range above 20,000 vps. This is why dogs can hear higher-pitched sounds than humans can, and they can detect sounds which alert them to danger before the human ear can pick up the same sound. This is a great asset for herding or guard work, alerting dogs to danger to their charges which might go undetected if wind conditions prevented detection by scent.

good chance that you will have the same type of dog, regardless of how much effort you put forth. However, breeders and owners contribute to the development of their dog's personality with love, attention, basic training, and discipline, all of which help him to achieve his optimum character development.

A Belgian should not show fear or shyness; he should be observant and vigilant with strangers, but not apprehensive. With those he knows well, he should be affectionate and friendly.

Belgians are a spirited breed, yet they are sensitive and respond well to commands. They adapt well to training, but do not respond well to rough treatment. If they understand what is expected of them they are willing and eager to please.

EYES

The Belgian Sheepdog Standard calls for brown eyes, preferably dark brown, of medium size, slightly almond-shaped, and not protruding. There are no statistics that indicate a dark-eyed dog can see any better than one with a light eye. The color choice may have its origins in the idea of light reflection. When referring to the color of the eye, we actually are referring to the color of the iris, for the pupil is always black. It is the retina, not the iris, that reflects the light.

Many people think that a light-eyed dog, in a breed that is supposed to have dark eyes, is not as stable in temperament as the dark-eyed dog. The light eye is more noticeable in a black dog because the contrast between the eyes and the black coat gives the dog a more piercing stare and not the soft, friendly look that is characteristic of the Belgian Sheepdog.

TEETH

Needless to say, a full set of teeth—twenty upper, twenty-two lower—is to be desired. Belgians can have either an even or a scissor bite. If the incisors meet squarely, one above the other, the dog has a level or even bite. When the incisors slide past one another, the outside face of the lower just grazing the inside face of the upper, the dog has a scissor bite.

The even bite has many advantages for dogs that herd sheep. The dogs can and will pinch or nip the sheep and the even bite is not as destructive as the scissor bite when the dogs have to use force in directing the sheep. The scissor bite has its advantage in police work, because it gives the dogs a more secure grip. The scissor bite does not wear down the teeth as fast as does an even bite in which the teeth hit together directly every time.

Many people are confused about overshot and undershot bites. The overshot mouth has the upper incisor striking in front of the lower, while the undershot mouth has the lower striking in front of the upper.

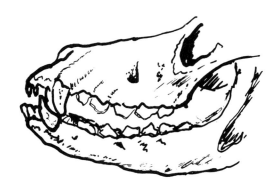

Faulty undershot bite. Front teeth of lower jaw projecting beyond front teeth of upper jaw when mouth is closed.

Faulty overshot bite. Front teeth of upper jaw overlap and do not touch front teeth of lower jaw when mouth is closed.

TORSO

The torso starts with the neck, and the Standard calls for a well-muscled neck. Since the head is important to the neck, we cannot talk about one without also discussing the muscles necessary for locomotion. The head contains many muscles, such as those that raise or retract the ears, and the muscles that govern the eyes, but there are two muscles that are most important as far as function is concerned. The major one, *masseter*, is fastened to the lower jaw, just in front of the socket and the upper skull, and just above the back teeth, where it spreads out in a fan shape. It has more power than any other head muscle and is the biting muscle. The other important muscle, *zygomaticus*, is a long strip that extends from the cartilage of the ear in front of the lower jaw. It causes the jaw to retract.

There is also a cervical ligament that has flexible stretch and retraction. This ligament supports the neck and governs head carriage. It stabilizes the base attachment of the muscles that move the leg forward and rotate the shoulder blade as the leg moves backward. The cervical ligament has two parts: The first cord runs along the top of the ligament from the base of the skull back to the fourth vertebra, where it becomes part of the spinal ligament; the second part is like a web running back from all except two of the neck vertebrae. A well-muscled neck is very important to good movement.

The head and neck of a dog have another very important function. Together they shift the center of gravity from side to side and help maintain equilibrium. When a dog is running, he extends his neck and head forward, putting more weight forward, which increases his speed. When a dog comes to an abrupt stop from high speed, he will throw his head and neck high. This shifts the center of gravity backward and serves as a braking action. If the dog stopped abruptly with his head low and forward, he would probably fall.

The vertebral column is divided into five sections: neck, withers, back, croup, and tail. The withers are slightly higher than the neck, and slope into the back, which must be level, straight, and firm from withers to hip joints. There are seven vertebrae in the neck. The first two differ in shape from the others and allow the head to move freely. The next five divide the neck into two parts, with separate sets of muscles attached to each part. This is the "pole" or arch in the back of the neck. This is functional and also gives the dog the proud carriage which we admire so much.

There are thirteen vertebrae (dorsal) that make up the withers and the back. The eight that compose the withers have the longest vertical spires and provide anchorage for the shoulder muscles. The five vertebrae that make up the back gradually change in shape from those of the withers to those of the loin (lumbar). There are seven vertebrae in the loin, and these have transverse prongs. The croup has three vertebrae (sacral) which are fused together for firmer anchorage to the pelvis. The number of vertebrae in the tail varies.

The back must be level, straight, and firm, since the power of the hindquarters must travel to the forequarters through the spinal column. Power can be transmitted faster and more forcefully in a straight line than through a convex curvature of the back (which is known as a roach back), or through a concave curvature of the back (commonly called a swayback).

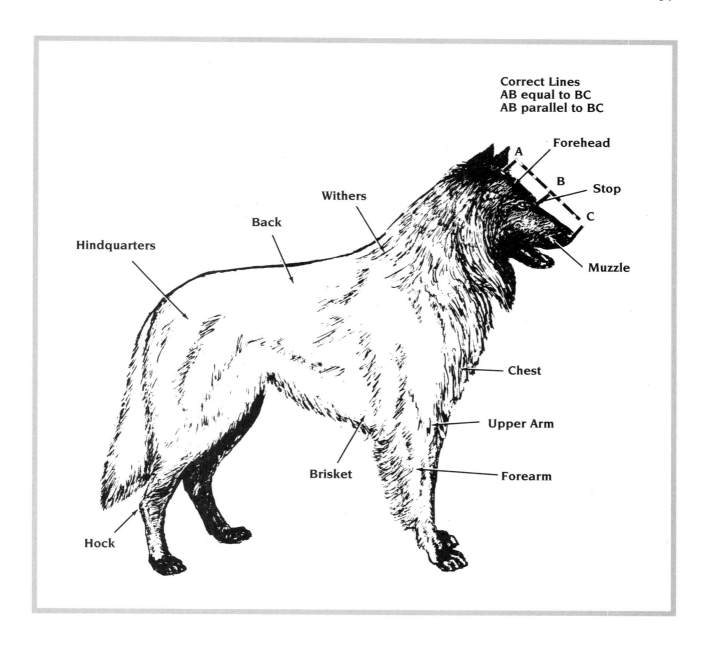

The concave curvature which usually occurs as a result of a combination of bad formation of the withers, a long back, and weak ligaments, diminishes the dog's endurance and speed.

The back connects the fore and aft of the dog much like a bridge over which forward movements are conveyed from behind. It must be strong, with thick, hard, conditioned muscles, since it does a double duty of connecting and carrying, and works as the medium of transmitting power.

THE LOIN

The loin is one of the most misunderstood parts of a dog, but is a very important factor in appearance. The loin is located between the rib section and the croup and is comprised of seven vertebrae. These vertebrae are wider than the dorsal vertebrae, and their spines' processes, or fingers, are short, thin, and wide. The spines' processes incline forward to give better support to the rearing muscles. Their pull is backward, just the opposite of those in the shoulder. The loin does not have support from other bones of the frame, but is more like a bridge between two working parts of the dog's body.

Most Standards call for a slightly arched loin (for strength), since this section has little support other than muscles. This slight arch must not be confused with a roach back, which will draw the loin up. The loin section is relatively short, broad, and strong, but should blend smoothly into the back. The loin must be long enough for flexibility but short enough for strength. This is achieved by depth. The girth of the loin is the result of solid, hard muscles, which are so important to the support of this section. Short, strong loins are essential for endurance. A loin that is too long can be compared to a long span of bridge lacking proper support.

The croup is a continuation of the back and should be of medium length, sloping gradually. This sounds simple enough, but these few words hold a great impact on the function of the rear end of a dog and the action of the hind legs. A gradual slope from the pelvic bone to the set-on of the tail is desirable. A dog with a level croup which is too short has a tendency to carry his tail high in the air. He will lack steadiness and the hindquarters will step short, with lack of thrust, which will restrict the gait. A dog that has a steep croup is hampered in his stride and lacks balance. The motion of the hind legs as this dog moves is more upward than forward. The transference of the motion through the back is interrupted, and the poor follow-through detracts from smoothness and power of motion.

A correctly formed croup will influence the proper carriage of the tail.

CHEST

The chest is not broad, but deep. The lowest point should reach the elbow, forming a smooth ascendant curve to the abdomen.

The thorax should be capacious with plenty of room for heart and lungs. This must be achieved by a wide spring of rib at the junction of rib and spine, followed by an abrupt drop of the rib. This leaves the side of the dog flat, and offers maximum capacity with the least impediment to the action of the shoulder and leg.

Pose your dog in the correct position, place your hand slightly behind the elbow, and see for yourself if it is flat enough for the elbow to pass in a straight line. If there is a bulge and the leg is too tight against the body, you can be sure there is not enough clearance for the smooth passage of the leg.

There is a great difference between a well-sprung rib and a barrel-shaped rib. The barrel rib follows a circular line of the same relative degree from the spinal column to the junction with the brisket. Barrel-shaped ribs may look impressive, but they will cause the feet to toe in and the elbows to spring outward.

A small breast, without depth, will cause the front legs to draw in at the elbows, and the feet will turn out in an east-west position. This will prevent the feet and legs from traveling in a proper forward movement.

FOREQUARTERS

The forequarters develop no power of their own. Their main function is to lift the front and absorb the power transmitted from the hindquarters through the spinal column. Incorrect shoulders that do not permit the dog to reach far enough in front to keep the front feet out of the way of the hind feet will cause the dog to crab, or side-step. The hind feet have to pass the forefeet in some way, and stepping to the side is a way of least resistance. A dog with a straight shoulder will not have adequate length of neck. The proud arch of the neck will be lost, and this will affect the gait because a straight shoulder shifts the center of gravity and makes the maintenance of equilibrium difficult. If the shoulder does not allow sufficient reach to take care of the drive from the hindquarters, too much shock will be put on the front. Nature, in trying to compensate, will thicken the muscles, and the result will be "loaded" shoulders. The muscles thicken to gain strength and the top is forced outward, bringing the shoulder point in and the elbows out. It is of little value to have well-angulated hindquarters to propel the animal without having sufficient angle of shoulder to absorb the stride. A dog with straight shoulders usually has a mincing gait, or may raise its front feet high in a hackney action which fools a lot of people. It may look like a spirited gait, but the dog is only trying to extend beyond his normal reach. This constant pounding will, in time, result in loaded shoulders. A dog that is balanced on both ends, even though the ends are not particularly good, will move better than one that is good on one end and bad on the other.

The length of the layback (the angle of the shoulder blade as compared with the vertical) determines the length of reach, and the dog cannot reach any farther. The better the layback, the smoother a dog can run with the least amount of effort.

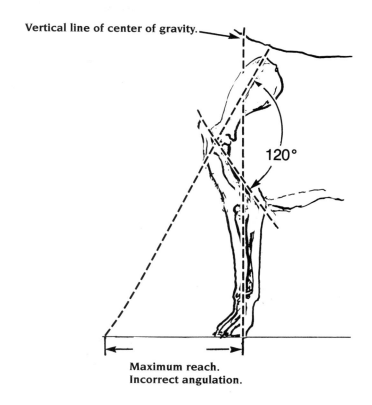

Maximum reach.
Incorrect angulation.

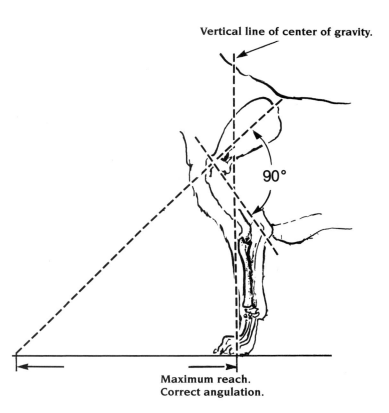

Maximum reach.
Correct angulation.

East-west feet. Leg bones turned out. Weak ligaments. This is called "French standing," or "dancing master's position."

Fiddle front. Forelegs out at elbows, pasterns close, and feet turned out.

Toed-in stance. Toes turned in. Forelegs out at elbows. Elbows extended, protruding out from natural line of body from shoulder joint to foot when viewed from front. Breast too broad.

Narrow front, lacking depth of chest.

Front too wide.

Good front. Legs straight, strong, parallel to each other. Toes close knit, well arched, and compact.

LEGS AND FEET

Two very important parts of a dog's anatomy are his legs and the feet. The legs should be straight, strong, and parallel to each other. The leg bone is oval rather than round. Development (length and substance) should be well proportioned. Length and substance well-proportioned to the size of the dog is very important. A dog that reaches maximum height but that has small, frail legs will look, and is, out of balance. There must be balance regardless of height. A dog that is undersized, with heavy bone and short legs, will look cumbersome, and his movement will lack the light, springy action characteristic of the Belgian Sheepdog. An unbalanced condition is not only offensive to the eye; it affects all other working parts of the body. Without balance, other functional parts of the framework will be under stress and deterioration of these parts will affect the working ability of the dog.

The pastern (that is, the region of the foreleg between the "wrist" and the digits) should be of medium length, strong,

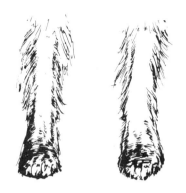

Good feet, with compact toes, well arched and muscular.

Weak, flat feet, with elongated toes and thin pads.

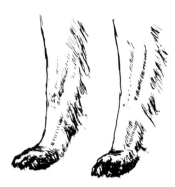

Splayed feet, lacking compactness and strength and easily injured. Feet are spread wide apart, with little or no arch.

Good conformation. Compact feet with pasterns slightly bent to absorb shock.

Weak pasterns which will not support weight of shoulder assembly, putting stress on leg muscles and tendons on back of leg.

Straight pasterns, indicating a straight shoulder assembly. Little or no shape to bones between pastern joint and foot.

and slightly sloped. The pasterns of a Belgian will not be sloped as much as those of a German Shepherd, but a Belgian with a good layback of shoulder should have slightly sloped pasterns. A dog with straight shoulders or a short upper arm will have pasterns that are straight up and down. A line starting from the center of the shoulder blade, vertical to the ground, should pass through the large pad of the foot. If the pasterns are weak, this will not be the case.

When we talk about weak pasterns, we must also talk about bad feet; when we talk about bad feet, we find weak pasterns. It is hard to say which comes first. The feet may hold up better if they have more support, or if the feet are good to begin with, then the pasterns may be able to stand constant strain. Which is to blame makes no difference, for the results will be the same; the dog will not have the endurance that is needed in a working dog.

The feet should be round (cat-footed), with the toes curved closely together and well padded. The thickness of the pads depends to a certain degree on inheritance, but the type of terrain that the dog is exposed to makes a great difference. Thin pads will not hold up for long on a working dog.

Cat-foot—correct on Belgian Sheepdog. Deep, short, round, compact foot. Short third digits bring toes closer to heel pad.

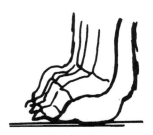

Hare-foot—faulty on Belgian Sheepdog. Longer third digits result in elongated foot.

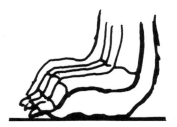

Conditioning will help, but not much. The pads must be thick to cushion the shock of normal movement. Even a dog with good, thick pads can develop sore, tender feet if he is exposed to rough terrain after spending his life on a smooth lawn or thick carpet. If a dog is to be used as a working dog, his feet should be conditioned on crushed rock, gravel, or some other hard surface before he is worked on rough, uneven ground.

Elongated toes are a serious problem. There is no way to develop a cat-foot from a foot with elongated toes. Proper terrain helps some, but the length of the toes is still there and the dog is going to have splayed feet. Too little emphasis has been put on the elimination of poor feet from breeding programs. Since the feet support the entire dog when he is moving or standing still, eliminating poor feet should be an important factor in a breeding program. Compact feet add to the overall appearance of a dog, besides being less subject to injury when the dog is working or just running in the yard.

HINDQUARTERS

The hindquarters play a different part than the forequarters. Of necessity, the muscles have to be broad and heavy in order to give the thrust that transmits power through the back to the forequarters. The hind assembly is not designed to support weight. It is designed to generate power for speed and normal movement. Through the stretching of muscles and the thrust from the ground, the hind legs provide forward momentum which is transferred to the forequarters through the back; this is called the "follow-through."

The hind legs are made up of many parts which affect the dog's gait—the upper part of the thigh joined to the pelvis, the second thigh, and the metatarsus joined with the hind foot. The skeleton is made up of the pelvic bones joined with the hip joint, the femur, the tibia and the fibula, and the bones of the hock, under which there are the powerful bones of the metatarsus and toes.

The pelvis provides an attachment for a large number of muscles which are important for motion. The power of its construction and the correctness of its position are of great importance to the efficiency of the dog. The gradual slope of the croup from the pelvic bones to the set-on of the tail is important to the hindquarters assembly. This construction and the slope of the croup determine the extension of the hindquarters while the dog is in motion. The size and formation of the head, or ball, of the femur play an important role in smooth action. A deep socket with a well-formed head is a necessity. A malformed head or too shallow a socket is a characteristic of the dreaded hip dysplasia that plagues so many breeds. Also, a socket that is too deep, so that the head of the femur cannot move freely, will cause a restricted gait. This condition is like a piece of machinery where a joint or socket is so tight that it cannot move in rhythm with other mechanical parts, which in turn causes a breakdown in other parts that would perform normally if the timing was right.

It is easy to understand how a shallow socket, one that does not have the depth to let the femoral head rotate without slipping out, can cause constant damage not only to the head but to the inadequate socket as well. The gristle-like capsule that surrounds this area thickens to hold the femur in place. The femur head moves farther from the hip socket, becoming more deformed. Nature, in trying to compensate, builds up calcium deposits which in time cause the area to become inflamed and painful. This will lead to an arthritic condition, and it will be difficult for the dog to get up and down.

The Standard states that Belgians do not have *extreme* angulation, which is true, since they are supposed to resemble a square, but this does not mean that they do not have to have *good* angulation. In order to move forward at any speed that is required, they must have thrust from the hind legs to transmit power through the back to the forequarters. The bone extending from the hock joint should be broad and deep, indicating great strength. From the hock joint to the foot the metatarsus should be short. If the metatarsus is too long the dog will lack endurance and quickness of movement.

The hind feet have the same requirements as the front feet, but the hind feet must be proportionately stronger and longer, because their function is to impart a powerful push to the body. Dewclaws, which sometimes occur on the lower third of the inner part of the metatarsus, will interfere with stance

Good hocks, broad and deep. Firm and well molded, never spongy or weak.

Bandy legs or bowlegs.

Cow hocks, pointing inward toward one another. Leg action is on bias and loses efficiency.

Hocks too close and too long. Weak.

and gait because the feet will have to adopt a wide gait in order to miss the dewclaws. This is most noticeable when a dog is single tracking. Dewclaws should be removed at an early age, when they are only loose excrescences with a nail, and only in rare cases joined to the bone by cartilaginous tissues. If left until maturity they not only hamper gait but are easily torn on rocks and rough ground.

COAT

The guard hairs of the Belgian Sheepdog's coat must be long, well fitting, straight, and abundant—not silky or wiry. The desired coat texture should be of medium harshness, although the texture can vary according to the climate in which the dogs are raised. Dogs raised in mild, warm climates will not carry the same coat as dogs raised in cold climates. Dogs that live outside will grow coats to protect themselves from elements, and the undercoat will be denser. The guard hairs will be of a harder texture for protection in rain and snow. Belgians will sometimes curl up in snow to sleep and practically become covered with it, but if you examine the undercoat you will notice it is not wet.

It is not advisable for a dog that has spent most of his time in the house suddenly to be made to spend much time outside, for nature will not have had a chance to provide the proper insulation.

COLOR

Black dogs have a common problem. Since Belgians are working dogs and spend most of their time outside, they can, and many do, have a tendency to get sunburned in the heat of summer. A reddish cast to the coat is not uncommon. This condition is seasonal and should not be confused with poor pigmentation.

GAIT

When we talk about the proper functions of the different parts of a dog, we are actually talking about how the parts affect the gait of the dog. A dog that is built properly should move correctly, but that does not always hold true because of the condition of the muscles. The dog must have exercise to strengthen the muscles and to achieve his potential. Muscles provide the power and force that make motion possible. Muscles are made up of fleshy elastic bands and nerve tissue. They lengthen and contract to move the bones to which they are attached. Each portion of the body has its own particular muscles that perform in unison with other sets of muscles to propel the dog forward.

First, we should understand a little about what happens in different types of gait. The *stride* is the distance traveled from one paw mark to the next by the same pad. *Timing* refers to the number of changes which take place in support of the body through the legs. *Right and left diagonal* describes the support when one front foot and the opposite back foot move together. This applies to either the right or left foot, whichever moves first.

The *walk* is a four-beat movement, in which all four legs move one after another. This gives four different combinations of weight support. Usually at least two, if not three, legs support the body at all times. As a general rule, the dog will lead off with the front foot. This permits the front foot to act a split second ahead of the back and will give clearance for the back foot; otherwise the dog will have to sidestep to miss the front foot. If he starts with the left front foot he will follow with the right rear foot, and vice versa.

The *trot* shows the faults and good points of a dog better than any other gait. The trot is a two-beat gait and brings into play the opposite front and rear legs moving in unison with each other. To have proper support, the front foot must move slightly in advance of the corresponding back foot and will

Coming.

Going away.

Correct single tracking. Note that support leg is placed directly under center line of gravity.

leave room for the back foot to advance. Watch the withers when a dog is in a trot. The withers should not bounce. Dogs seldom walk but usually are in either a slow trot or a fast trot. This gait is more suited to different types of terrain and provides greater endurance when traveling long distances.

The *pace* is a "fatigue" gait, and one to avoid in the show ring. The pace is a two-beat lateral gait. The left front leg and the left rear leg move in unison, as do the right legs. This makes a shift of laterals from one side to another. This is an easy gait and less tiresome than the trot, and when a dog is tired he will resort to this gait in order to ease the toll of fatigue. Since this gait is a shifting from one side to the other it tends to ease the shock on the forequarters as the hindquarters help support the weight, but at the same time it gives a swing to the body which is not pleasing to the eye. A dog is in the show ring for such a short time that he should not have to resort to the fatigue gait; if he does, there is something wrong, either in his physical construction or in his condition. Sometimes the handler moves in an in-between stride himself and forces the dog to match his stride.

The *gallop* is a gait that a dog uses when he has a need for increased speed. The major muscles which draw the rear legs backward are on the back side of the thigh. These muscles are commonly referred to as the rearing muscles. The rearing muscles are the important tools in this gait. The thrust is the force that sends the body forward, and is taken up by the extended front legs. The weight of the whole body is carried by these muscles as they lift the front. If we know what makes these sudden bursts of speed possible, and how important the hocks and the rearing muscles are, we can see the need for strong hindquarters and back to maintain speed for as long as is necessary. This is especially important in any working dogs used for herding. They must be able to hold their speed until their charges can be headed off,

GLOSSARY OF TERMS RELATING TO CONFORMATION

Almond eyes—The set of the eye is almond-shaped rather than round.
Apple head—Rounded topskull, more humped toward the center.
Butterfly nose—Parti-color nose, dark with flesh-colored markings.
Crabbing—A sidewise movement of the body at an angle to the line of progress.
Dewclaws—Extra claw or functionless fifth toe on inside of leg.
Flat croup—Croup with little or no slope downward from the backline.
Flat-sided—Ribs relatively flat in midsection.
Frog-face—Extended nose with receding jaw, usually overshot.
Gay tail—Tail carried high above the backline.
Goose rump—Too steep or sloping croup.
Hackney action—The high lifting of the front feet as in a hackney horse.
Layback—The angle of the shoulder blade.
Lippy—Loose lips that do not fit tightly.
Loaded shoulders—Shoulder blades under which the muscles have been overdeveloped so blades push outward from the body.
Loin—The region of the body on both sides of the vertebral column between the lower ribs and the hindquarters.
Out at elbows—Elbows protruding from natural line of the body when viewed from the front.
Out at shoulder—Blade-set that places the joints too far apart for proper movement.
Pigeon-breast—Chest with protruding breastbone.
Roach back—Pronounced convex curve of backline toward loin. (Sometimes called carp back.)
Shelly—Shallow, narrow body, very little spring to ribs.
Sickle hocked—In a standing position, the hock joint is bent at an angle.
Sickle tail—Tail carried high in a semicircle.
Snipey face—Pointed, weak muzzle lacking in bone formation.
Spring of ribs—Curve of ribs for lung and heart capacity.
Swayback—Concave curve in backline between withers and hipbones.
Undershot—Front teeth of lower jaw projecting beyond front teeth of upper jaw when mouth is closed.
Wry mouth—Lower jaw is not aligned with upper jaw.
Weaving—Crossing of forefeet or hind feet when in motion.

and still have some reserve to call on in case of another change in direction.

In a fast trot the Belgian Sheepdog will single track, meaning the legs both front and rear converge toward the dog's center line of gravity. The backline should remain firm and level, parallel to the line of motion, with no crabbing. A dog in a fast gait cannot maintain his equilibrium unless his legs converge toward the center line of gravity. This is the only way he can move in a straight line, without his body swaying from side to side.

All herding dogs will single track in a fast gait, for they can then cover more ground with the least amount of effort. Even people single track when they walk or run. If you are in doubt about the mechanics of single tracking, go out in the yard and run in the normal manner, and watch your feet come in toward the center of gravity. Then place your feet about twelve inches apart, and

Ch. Bel-Reve's Pistolero bred by Cathy and Bill Daugherty. Photo © Ashbey Photography.

go forward with your feet moving in a straight line. You can feel the pounding motion and your body will sway from side to side. It is easy to see why you could not run very far and maintain speed without physical exhaustion.

FAULTS

Any deviation from the Standard is classified as a fault. The extent to which any deviation affects the working ability of the dog determines whether the fault is considered major or minor.

Breeders must know the Standard and understand the function of all parts of the body in order to know to what extent their dogs deviate from the Standard. Even if a dog never does a day's work in his life, he still has to move. If he is put together right, he will live his life with a minimum of body stress. A good example is the Veteran Class in a Specialty show. We see dogs moving with great ease at the age of twelve years and older. These dogs were built correctly. Bad qualities as well as good qualities will affect the breed and the ability of future generations to function properly. Dog breeding is a responsibility that should not be taken lightly if you love your breed.

Seven-week-old Cheyenne enjoyed playing in a small basket. Owned by Frank and Artice Mainville.

CHAPTER FIVE

For Better or Worse, He's in Your Care

BELGIANS ADAPT WELL TO MANY different situations and living conditions. Your Belgian will probably prefer being both an outdoor and indoor dog. He needs space to exercise, but likes spending time with the family inside as well. A fenced yard or run is almost essential for this breed unless you enjoy early morning and late evening walks. While not prone to overactivity or problem behavior when kept as a house dog, like most breeds in the Herding Group, Belgians have plenty of energy and need an outlet for it. A daily romp in the yard or park, or a long walk, will fulfill this need. Obedience or agility training or actual work such as herding and tracking are helpful for keeping the Belgian's energy channeled into constructive behavior.

HOUSING

Every dog should have a bed of his own, snug and warm, where he can retire undisturbed when he wishes to nap. Especially with a small puppy, it is desirable to have the bed arranged so the dog can be securely confined at times, safe and contented. If the puppy is taught early in life to stay quietly in his box at night or when the family is out, the habit will carry over to adulthood and will benefit both dog and master.

Although the Belgian Sheepdog is a hardy breed and can live outside, he should never be banished to a damp, cold basement, but should be quartered in an out-of-the-way corner close to the center of family activity. His bed can be a plastic airline crate, a simple rectangular wooden box, or a heavy paper carton cushioned with a clean cotton rug or towel. Actually, the latter is ideal for a new puppy, for it is snug, easy to clean, and expendable. A "door" can be cut on one side of the box for easy access, but it should be placed in such a way that the dog can still be confined when desirable.

A shipping crates makes excellent indoor quarters. It is lightweight but strong, provides adequate air circulation, yet is snug and warm and easily cleaned. A crate is ideal for the owner who plans to take his dog along when he travels because the dog will willingly

An airline crate makes an excellent "den" for a puppy when placed in a quiet corner near— but out of the mainstream of family activity.

Your adult Belgian may prefer sleeping in a dog bed or on a rug to a crate. If you prefer to switch to this type of bed, wait until your dog is reliably housebroken.

Crates come in various sizes to suit various breeds of dogs. For reasons of economy, the size selected should be adequate for use when the dog is full grown. A No. 400 is adequate for an adult Belgian. If the area seems too large when your puppy is small, a temporary cardboard partition can be installed to limit the area he occupies. For convenience and to enhance the dog's sense of security, keep food and water dishes in the same general area as the crate.

Mature dogs can be kept in a garage with a dog door that opens into the yard, or in a chain-link kennel run at least 6 x 12 feet with a good doghouse. An all-weather dog house must have a raised floor and either a flap over the door or an entryway that prevents drafts from entering the house. Plenty of shade must be provided in hot weather, either from trees and bushes or from a shade cloth or tarpaulin over the top of the run. Be sure to spend plenty of "family time" with the dog and do not relegate your Belgian to his run day and night without individualized attention, play, and training sessions. Temperament and behavior problems can develop rapidly when a dog is neglected in this way.

TOYS AND CHEWING

Belgians, like all puppies, are inclined to chew and need something of their own to chew on. You can purchase rawhide bones, pig ears, cow hooves, and other processed sinew and bone products at your local pet store. Rubber chew toys, balls, dental ropes, and various kinds of toys abound, or you can make your own toys from an old piece of sheepskin, a knotted-up rope, used tennis balls, or stuffed toys without button eyes or noses. Boiled beef knucklebones are safe for your puppy.

stay in his accustomed bed during long automobile trips, and the crate can be taken inside motels or hotels at night, making the dog a far more acceptable guest.

Dog crates made of chromed metal or wood are also available, and some crates have tops covered with rubber matting that can be used for a grooming table. Anyone moderately handy with tools can construct a wooden crate.

Your local pet store will offer a variety of rawhide chews, including rawhide bones and sticks, pig snouts, cow ears, etc.

Toys keep your puppy happy and busy. Be sure to remove dangerous button eyes and other objects that the puppy might swallow accidently.

Rope, balls, and tug toys are other good choices that will keep your puppy occupied and distract him from chewing on your favorite slippers.

Keep some of these toys available to your young Belgian all during the teething stage. Otherwise, he may chew on something of yours!

Unwanted chewing is easier to prevent than to cure. Keep shoes, socks and other items your puppy might want to carry around or chew safely out of reach. If he does pick up the wrong object, distract him and offer him a favorite chew toy of his own.

Adult dogs will enjoy balls, chewies, a Frisbee that you toss, or a favorite stuffed toy. They can be taught to put their toys away in a storage box where they can get them when they want to play. Games of chase and retrieve are a good way to exercise a house dog.

The variety of dog food available in a local PetsMart store is simply overwhelming. Learn to read and compare labels carefully or ask your veterinarian or breeder to recommend a good brand and stay with it.

NUTRITION AND FEEDING

When your Belgian reaches six months of age, feeding him twice a day is sufficient. For mature dogs, one large meal a day is usually sufficient, although some owners prefer to give two meals. As long as the dog enjoys optimum health and is neither too fat nor too thin, the number of meals a day makes little difference.

The amount of food required for mature dogs will vary. A mature dog usually eats slightly less than he did as a growing puppy. Most dogs do better if the food is increased slightly during the winter months and reduced somewhat during hot weather when the dog is less active.

The main food elements required by dogs are proteins, fats, and carbohydrates. Vitamins A, B complex, D, and E are essential, as are ample amounts of calcium and iron. The most important nutrient is protein and it must be provided every day of the dog's life, for it is essential for normal daily growth and replacement of body tissues burned up in daily activity. Preferred animal protein products are beef, lamb, chicken, and boned fish. The "meat meal" used in some commercial foods is made from scrap meat processed at high temperatures and then dried. It is not as nutritious as fresh meat, but in combination with other protein products, it is an acceptable ingredient in the dog's diet.

Dog foods manufactured by well-known and reputable companies are nutritionally sound and are offered in sufficient variety of flavors, textures, and consistencies that most dogs will find them tempting and satisfying. A high-quality dry kibble labeled as a "complete" diet is a good choice. Ask the breeder what the puppy was eating before you took him home and make any change in brand or type of food gradually. Most breeders recommend that you feed a formula designed especially for puppies until the dog is six months of age, then switch gradually to an adult food. If the puppy is a picky eater, adding warm water, a little milk, or cottage cheese may make the food more palatable.

Vegetables supply additional proteins, vitamins, and minerals and, by providing fiber, are of value in overcoming constipation. Raw or cooked carrots, celery, lettuce, beets, asparagus, tomatoes, and cooked spinach may be used. They should always be chopped or ground well and mixed with the other food. Various combinations may be used, but a good home-mixed ration for the mature dog consists of two parts of meat and one each of vegetables and dog meal (or cereal product).

Fiber is an important part of the diet. A dry food that is too low in fiber can

Keep fresh water available at all times. This puppy shares a water bowl with the family cat.

cause an increase in the risk of disease or infection. Diets consisting only of highly absorbable ingredients can lead to instestinal disturbances. Too high a fiber level will either speed up digestion and cause diarrhea or slow it down, causing deficiencies in the amount of certain nutrients. Dry dog food should list "crude fiber" in the range of 3 to 5 percent. The type of fiber is also important. Look for fiber that is digested at a moderate rate, such as beet pulp, in the ration. Pectin, carob bean gum and other gums break down too rapidly, while cellulose fiber is not digested at all.

Candy and other sweets are taboo, for the dog has no nutritional need for them and if he is permitted to eat them, he will usually eat less of foods he requires. Also taboo are fried foods, highly seasoned foods, and extremely starchy foods, for the dog's digestive tract is not equipped to handle them.

Bones provide little nourishment, although gnawing bones helps make the teeth strong and helps to keep tartar from accumulating. Beef bones, especially large knucklebones, are best. Fish, poultry, and chop bones should *never* be given to dogs since they have a tendency to splinter and can puncture the dog's digestive tract.

Clean, fresh, cool water is essential and an adequate supply should be available twenty-four hours a day. During hot weather the drinking pan should be emptied and refilled at frequent intervals.

Feeding the Breeding Animal

Before a bitch is bred, make sure that she is in optimum condition—slightly on the lean side rather than fat. The bitch in whelp is given much the same diet she was fed prior to breeding, with slight increases in amounts of meat, liver, and dairy products. Beginning about six weeks after breeding, she should be fed two meals per day rather than one, and the total daily intake gradually increased. Some bitches in whelp require as much as fifty percent more food than they consumed normally. Do not permit the bitch to become fat, for whelping problems are more likely to occur in overweight dogs. Your veterinarian may suggest cod-liver oil and dicalcium phosphate supplements until after the puppies are weaned.

The dog used only occasionally for breeding will not require a special diet, but he should be well fed and maintained in optimum condition. A dog used frequently might require a slightly increased amount of food, but his basic diet will require no change if his general health is good and his flesh is firm and hard.

EXERCISE

Because he is an active, working type of dog, you may think your Belgian doesn't need regular exercise. While he is young, that may be true—he may get plenty of exercise just running, jumping, and playing. However, as he matures, your dog will benefit greatly—both healthwise and behaviorally—from regular exercise. This can be long walks of a mile or more, jogging beside a bicycle, retrieving a ball or Frisbee, or doing some type of work like tracking or herding at least three times a week. Your Belgian will enjoy hiking with you and he is large enough to carry a backpack with lunch and supplies. In fact, an adult Belgian should be able to carry six or seven pounds in his pack. However, he must be conditioned gradually. Don't take your house dog out for a ten-mile hike on the first nice spring weekend when he hasn't walked a mile in two months! Regular, planned exercise sessions will keep him in shape for those impromptu activities you and he both will enjoy.

EXERCISE CHOICES FOR YOUR BELGIAN

- Play ball. Teach your dog to retrieve.
- Throw a Frisbee, canvas disk, or Go-Frrrs toy.
- Take him for a swim in the lake.
- Toss a floating object for him to retrieve from the water.
- Take your dog for a hike in the hills.
- Jog around the neighborhood with your dog, or consider entering a race for dogs and their owners.
- Let the kids romp, roll, and tumble with him.
- Take your dog along on a bike ride.
- Have your dog pull you on skis or in a cart.
- Give him a treat ball filled with goodies so he exercises himself while you're away.
- Allow free time in a dog run or your backyard.
- Install a dog door so he can come and go into the yard at will.
- Take him for a romp at the park and let him romp on a long Flexi lead.
- Teach him to jump or do agility.
- Get involved in an active dog sport like tracking or herding.

Swimming is excellent exercise. These Belgian Sheepdog puppies are going for their first swimming lesson. Photo courtesy of owner, Kaye Hall.

Youth plus youth is a great combination for training and fun. Six-month-old Bel-Reve's Southern Cross goes for a walk in the park with Stefanie Ferraro.

CARING FOR THE OLDER BELGIAN

As your Belgian reaches seven years old or so, he will become less active. He may gain too much weight or his appetite may decrease so he becomes too thin. It is necessary to adjust the diet in either case, for the dog will live longer and enjoy better health if he is maintained in trim condition. The simplest way to decrease or increase body weight is by decreasing or increasing the amount of fat in the diet. Many specialized dry and canned foods are available from your veterinarian or your local pet supply store. Read the labels and ask advice, then try some of the senior diets

Body condition chart. Maintaining your Belgian Sheepdog at his optimum weight and body condition is one of the best things you can do for his overall good health. Reprinted with permission from Purina Mills.

until you find one that works for your dog.

If an older dog becomes reluctant to eat, it may be necessary to coax him with special food he relishes. Warming the food will increase its aroma and usually will help to entice the dog to eat. If he still refuses, rubbing some of the food on the dog's lips and gums may stimulate interest. It may be helpful also to offer food in smaller amounts and increase the number of meals per day. Foods that are highly nutritious and easily digested are especially desirable for older dogs.

A Belgian Sheepdog will usually live until around twelve years old, and with good care and regular checkups, will occasionally live as long as sixteen years. If your dog's pedigree is free from hip dysplasia and PRA, your dog is unlikely to have a problem with arthritis or blindness, even in old age. You can help keep him active by adding a good joint supplement, available from your veterinarian, when he is approaching seven years of age and continuing it for the rest of his life. Joint supplements have been proven effective for increasing the mobility of older dogs (and people) and are safe if used according to the directions. New research indicates that antioxidants also help reduce the effects of aging in dogs and several pet food companies have started adding these to their ingredients. New developments even indicate that aging of the brain and problems such as incontinence can be controlled with food additives and nutrition. Ask your veterinarian and read current periodicals to keep abreast of similar exciting discoveries. As with humans, new technology and science will continue to help your pet age better and live longer.

Your Belgian Sheepdog can remain active even as he gets older. This is Ch. Belle Noire Laxson du Jet, CDX, TT "Jean Jean", at nine years and nine months of age. Owner, Kaye Hall.

Am. Can. Ch. Johnsondale's Jacque, CD, TT, HIC, CGC, TDI, at eight years old. Bred by Pat Johnson; owner, Ramona Kraft.

KEEPING YOUR BELGIAN HEALTHY

Simple measures of preventive care are always preferable to cures, which may be complicated and costly. Many of the problems which afflict dogs can be avoided quite easily by instituting good dog-keeping practices in connection with feeding and housing.

Cleanliness is essential in preventing the growth of disease-producing bacteria and other micro-organisms. All equipment, especially water and food dishes, must be kept immaculately clean. Cleanliness is also essential in controlling external parasites, which thrive in unsanitary surroundings

A healthy dog is alert, active, has clear eyes, light pink gums, and no nasal discharge. His coat is bright, shining, and not excessively oily. He has a good appetite and drinks moderate amounts of water.

Bright eyes, a shining coat, and an alert expression are signs of a healthy dog. Ch. Sherborne Heir Power, CD, enjoys time out in a fenced yard complete with roses and shade trees.

Symptoms of Illness

Symptoms of illness may be so obvious there is no question that the dog is ill, or so subtle that the owner isn't sure whether there is a change from normal or not. *Loss of appetite, lethargy* or general lack of interest in what is going on, and *vomiting* may be ignored if they occur singly and persist only for a day. However, in combination with other evidence of illness, such symptoms may be significant and the dog should be watched closely. *Abnormal bowel movements,* especially diarrhea or bloody stools, are causes for immediate concern. *Urinary abnormalities* may indicate infections, and bloody urine is always an indication of a serious condition. When a dog that has long been housebroken suddenly becomes incontinent, a veterinarian should be consulted, for he may be able to suggest treatment or medication that will be helpful.

More subtle signs of illness can include a sudden change of disposition or activity level, deep red or very pale gums, a very hot or cold nose, a dull, oily coat, or limping and/or stiffness. Dogs suffering from indigestion sometimes eat grass, apparently to induce vomiting and relieve discomfort.

Fever is a positive indication of illness and deviation from the normal temperature range of 100 to 102 degrees is cause for concern. Place the dog in a standing position to take his temperature. Coat the bulb of a digital or rectal thermometer with petroleum jelly, raise the dog's tail, insert the thermometer to approximately half its length, and hold it for the recommended time. Clean the thermometer with rubbing alcohol after each use.

Convulsions, often considered a symptom of worms, may result from a variety of causes including vitamin deficiencies, or playing to the point of exhaustion. A veterinarian should be consulted when a convulsion occurs as it may be a symptom of more serious illness.

Persistent coughing is often considered a symptom of worms, but may also indicate heart trouble—especially in older dogs.

Immunize Against Bacterial and Viral Diseases

Prevention is definitely the best medicine when it comes to the diseases that once commonly killed our canine companions. Breeders now routinely vaccinate puppies against parvovirus, distemper, hepatitis, leptospirosis, and often coronavirus and kennel cough. You as the new owner will be required to continue the series of puppy booster shots until full immunity is achieved. Your veterinarian will help you determine just what is needed.

Between four and six months of age your puppy will need his first rabies vaccination. A second booster is usually required.

Dogs are also now routinely protected from internal and external parasites (worms, fleas, etc.) and from the deadly infestation of the blood by heartworm larvae. Be sure to ask your veterinarian about all of these preventive medications when you take your puppy in for his first, and subsequent, checkups.

A heavy infestation with any type of worm is a serious matter and treatment must be started early and continued until the dog is free of the parasite or the dog's health will suffer seriously. Death could even result. On the other hand, promiscuous dosing for worms is dangerous and different types of worms require different treatment. So if you suspect your dog has worms, ask your veterinarian to

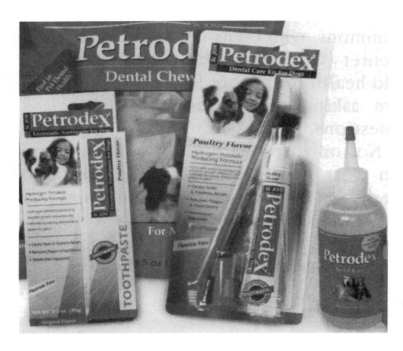

A variety of dental hygiene products are available. Use them regularly.

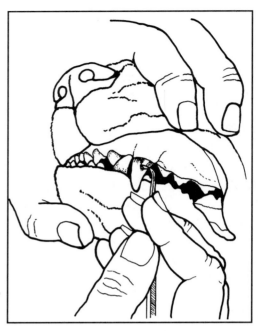

Clean your dog's teeth regularly, either by brushing or scaling.

Purchase a good quality nail clippers such as this one.

make a microscopic examination of the feces, and to prescribe appropriate treatment if evidence of worm infestation is found.

Other Health and Maintenance Concerns

Keeping the teeth clean is an ongoing task that begins when your dog is just a puppy. He should be accustomed to having his mouth opened and handled from an early age. When the baby canines loosen, you must check to see that there is room for the adult canine to come in. If an adult tooth is trying to come through but is wedged tightly against a baby tooth, your veterinarian should pull the juvenile tooth to make room for it; otherwise the new teeth may not be straight. You should learn to recognize the correct bite and number of teeth for your breed and have any abnormalities examined.

Your dog will need his teeth cleaned at regular intervals. Rawhide bones, special dental toys, and even special dog biscuits will help prevent the formation of tartar, but you will still need to brush your dog's teeth daily or scale them regularly with a special "tooth scaler." Mouth rinses, dental wipes, toothbrushes and paste, or anti-plaque-forming additives for your dog's drinking water are some of the daily methods of dental hygiene available for your dog. Tooth decay, receding, sore gums, or infection will cause heart disease and other serious problems, many of which are eventually responsible for the death of older dogs. If you don't keep your dog's teeth clean yourself, have your veterinarian clean the dog's teeth once a year or oftener as needed.

Nail clipping is a weekly chore unless your dog is very active or does a lot of running on cement or gravel. Purchase a good guillotine-style nail clippers and teach your dog to let you clip his nails while he is either standing on a grooming table or lying on his side on the floor. The Belgian's black nails make it difficult to see just how much to clip, so take only the tip of the nail each time, gradually shortening the nails over time until they no longer touch the floor when the dog walks. If you accidentally cut too deep and the nail bleeds, apply a styptic powder available from a grooming supply, or a little powdered alum. Hold it onto the nail tip until all bleeding ceases. If done frequently and without cutting into the "quick," clipping your pet's nails is as painless as trimming your own fingernails.

Clogged anal glands cause intense discomfort, which the dog may attempt to relieve by scooting himself along the floor on his haunches. These glands, located on either side of the anus, secrete a substance that enables the dog to expel the contents of the rectum. If they become clogged, they may give the dog an unpleasant odor and when neglected, serious infection may result. Contents of the glands can be easily expelled into a wad of cotton, which should be held under the tail with the left hand. Then, using the right hand, pressure should be exerted with the thumb on one side of the anus, the

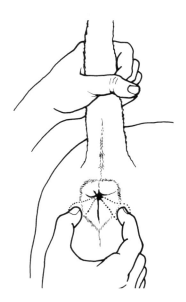

The anal glands are indicated by the dotted lines. Press on either side of the anal glands to express them. Then bathe your dog.

THE FIRST AID KIT

The following items should be kept on hand for caring for a sick or injured dog or for **administering first aid** for injuries:

- Antiseptic wash such a chlorhexidine
- Hydrogen peroxide (for wound cleaning or to induce vomiting)
- Cotton balls, cotton swabs, and gauze pads
- Rectal thermometer
- Tweezers
- Several syringes without needles
- Measuring spoons or container for liquid medication
- Adhesive tape and stretch bandages
- Burn ointment
- Panalog or triple antiseptic ointment
- Bag balm
- Boric acid solution (2%) or a commercial pet eye wash
- Surgical shampoo such as Betadine
- Small forceps
- Kaopectate or Pepto-Bismol
- Baby aspirin

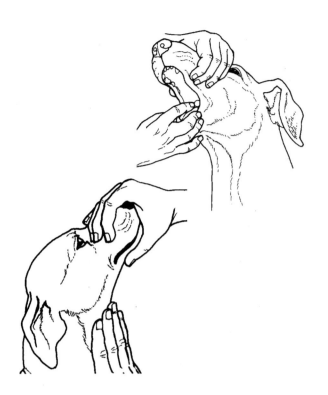

Place the pill far back on the dog's tongue. Close his mouth and stroke his throat to stimulate swallowing.

forefinger on the other. The normal secretion is brownish in color, with an unpleasant odor. The presence of blood or pus indicates infection and should be called to the attention of the veterinarian.

Eye problems of a minor nature—redness or occasional discharge—may be treated with a few drops of boric acid solution (2 percent) or salt solution (1 teaspoonful table salt to 1 pint sterile water), or with a commercial eye wash. Cuts on the eyeball, bruises close to the eyes, or persistent discharge should be treated only by a veterinarian.

Heat exhaustion is a serious (and often fatal) problem caused by exposure to extreme heat. Belgians, being a black-coated breed, will absorb a great deal of heat from the sunlight in summer. You can help your Belgian stay comfortable by providing plenty of shade and cool drinking water, providing a kid's pool for him to cool off in, and by either misting him with a spray bottle of cool water or covering him with a wet, white terrycloth towel when he is in the sun for an extended period, such as when waiting for a class at a show or trial.

Heat exhaustion most commonly occurs when a thoughtless owner leaves a dog in a closed vehicle without proper shade and ventilation. Even on a day when outside temperatures do not seem excessively high, heat builds up rapidly to an extremely high temperature in a closed vehicle parked in direct sunlight or even in partial shade. To prevent such a tragedy, never leave a dog unattended in a vehicle, even for a short time. During hot weather, whenever a dog is taken for a ride in an air-conditioned automobile, the cool air should be reduced gradually when nearing the destination, for the sudden shock of going from cool air to extremely hot temperatures can also result in shock and heat exhaustion.

Symptoms of heat exhaustion include rapid and difficult breathing and near or complete collapse. First aid treatment consists of sponging cool water over the body to reduce temperature as quickly as possible. Immediate medical treatment is essential in severe cases of heat exhaustion.

Care of the Ailing or Injured Dog

A dog that is seriously ill, requiring surgical treatment, transfusions, or intravenous feeding, must be hospitalized. One requiring less complicated treatment is better cared for at home, but it is essential that the dog be kept in a quiet environment. His bed should be in a room apart from family activity, yet close at hand so his condition can be checked frequently. Clean bedding and adequate warmth are essential, as are a constant supply of fresh, cool water, and foods to tempt the appetite.

Food offered the sick dog should be nutritious and easily digested. Meals should be smaller than usual and offered at more frequent intervals. If the dog is reluctant to eat, offer food he particularly likes. Warm it slightly to increase aroma and make it more tempting. Broth, rice, cottage cheese, yogurt, and cooked hamburger are some possible choices.

If special medication is prescribed, it may be administered in any one of several ways. A pill or small capsule may be concealed in a small piece of meat, which the dog will usually swallow with no problem. A large capsule may be given by holding the dog's mouth open, inserting the capsule as far as possible down the throat, then holding the mouth closed until the dog swallows. Liquid medicine should be measured into a small bottle or test tube. Then, if the corner of the dog's lip is pulled out while the head is tilted upward, the liquid can be poured between the lips and teeth, a small amount at a time. If he refuses to swallow, keeping the dog's head tilted and stroking his throat will usually induce swallowing.

Liquid medication may also be given by use of a syringe without a needle. The syringe is slipped into the side of the mouth and over the rise at the back of the tongue, and the medicine is "injected" slowly down the throat. This is especially good for medicine with a bad taste because the medicine does not touch the taste buds in the front part of the tongue. It also eliminates spills and guarantees that all the medicine goes in.

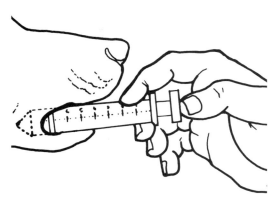

Liquid medication is administered more easily using a syringe with the needle removed.

It is nice to have a dog that will respond to voice control during an outing in the country. Ch. Sherborne Omega, CD, owned by Karla Huhn. Photo courtesy of Jill Sherer.

Chapter Six: The Well-Behaved Belgian

HOW WELL YOUR BELGIAN Sheepdog will behave depends a lot on the attention and training that he receives while he is growing up. Although each dog has personality quirks and idiosyncrasies that set him apart as an individual, dogs in general have two characteristics than can be utilized to advantage in training. The first is the dog's strong desire to please, which has been built up through centuries of association with man. The second is the innate quality of the dog's mentality. It has been proven conclusively that, while dogs have reasoning power, their learning ability is based on a direct association of cause and effect, so that they willingly repeat acts that bring pleasant results and discontinue acts that bring unpleasant results. So, in order to take fullest advantage of a dog's abilities, the trainer must make sure the dog understands a command, and then reward him when he obeys and correct him when he does wrong.

Commands should be as short as possible and should be repeated in the same way, day after day. Saying "Heel" one day and "Come here and heel" the next will confuse the dog. *Heel, sit, stand, stay, down,* and *come* are standard commands, and are preferable for a dog that may later be given advanced training.

Tone of voice is important, too. For instance, a coaxing tone will help cajole a young puppy into trying something new. Once an exercise is mastered, commands given in a firm, matter-of-fact voice give the dog confidence in his own ability. Praise expressed in an exuberant tone will tell the dog quite clearly that he has earned his master's approval, while a firm "No" indicates with equal clarity that he has done wrong.

Rewards for good performance include praising the dog lavishly, petting, or giving bits of food as a reward. Tidbits are effective only if the dog is hungry, of course. (If you smoke, be sure to wash your hands before each training session. The odor of nicotine is repulsive to dogs, and on the hands of a heavy smoker it may be so strong that the dog is unable to smell the tidbit.)

In order to be effective, a correction must be administered immediately, so that in the dog's mind there is a direct

One of the first things your puppy should learn is to recognize and respond when you call his name. This is Zula V. Siegestor, UDX, TT, CGC. Photo © Ann A. Palmer.

connection between his act and the correction. Voice corrections can be made under almost any circumstances, but you must never call the dog to you and then correct him. He will associate the correction with the fact that he has come and will become reluctant to respond in the future. If the dog is at a distance and doing something he shouldn't, you must go to him and scold him while he is still involved in wrongdoing. If this is impossible, ignore the offense until he repeats it and you can correct him properly.

BASIC TRAINING

Puppy classes that teach you and your puppy basic leash control and that socialize your puppy to other dogs, people, and distractions are available in most communities. Call your local humane shelter, kennel club, or training facility to find out if and when these are held. Most puppy classes are for puppies between three and four months of age when the class starts, so you need to find out about the next class soon after acquiring your puppy. Puppy classes are an excellent way to begin working with your puppy.

Informal obedience training, started at the age of six to eight months, will also provide a good background, and will also prepare your dog for any advanced training you may decide to do later.

The first thing to teach the dog is his name, so that whenever he hears it, he will immediately come to attention. Any time that you are near his box, talk to him, using his name repeatedly. During play periods, talk to your puppy, pet him and handle him. Hold him on his side or back for short periods, pick him up and carry him, or place him on a solid box or table. He must be conditioned so that he will not object to being handled by a veterinarian, show judge, or family friend.

Keep an eye on your puppy and try to distract him before he gets into mischief. Basic training in house manners begins the day the puppy enters his new home. Never give a new puppy the run of the house, but confine him to a box or small pen except for play periods when you can devote full attention to him.

As the puppy investigates his surroundings, watch him carefully and if he tries something he shouldn't, reprimand him with a scolding "No!" If he repeats the offense, scold him and confine him to his box, then praise him. Discipline must be prompt, consistent, and always followed with praise. Never tease the dog, and never allow others to

Watch your puppy closely as he explores his environment. Give him plenty of exposure to new places and situations. Photo © Kent and Donna Dannen.

do so. Kindness and understanding are essential to a pleasant, mutually rewarding relationship.

When your Belgian puppy is two to three months old he should start wearing a flat, narrow leather or nylon buckle collar. After he has worn it a week or so, attach a light nylon leash to the collar during play sessions and let the puppy walk around, dragging the leash behind him. Then hold the end of the leash and coax the puppy to come to you. Soon he will be fully accustomed to collar and leash, which will helpful when you start taking him outside during housebreaking.

Giving your puppy new and different experiences early in life will help him adapt and learn more easily when he is older. Start your training as soon as possible, but make it fun. Your dog is learning, whether you realize it or not. Be sure that he is learning what you want him to learn—don't leave it up to him. Working and playing together will create a bond between dog and master.

HOUSE TRAINING

Housebreaking can be accomplished in a matter of approximately two weeks provided you wait until the dog is mature enough to have some control over bodily functions. This usually occurs when the puppy is about four months old. Until that time, he should spend most of his day confined to a pen, with the floor covered with several thickness of newspapers so that he may relieve himself when necessary.

Either of two methods works well in housebreaking—the choice depends upon where you live. If you live in a house with a readily accessible yard, you will probably want to train the puppy to go outdoors. If you live in an apartment without easy access to a yard, you may decide to train him first to relieve himself on newspapers, and then teach the puppy to go outdoors when he has learned control.

In either case, arrange some means of confining the puppy indoors where you can watch him. Dogs are naturally clean animals, reluctant to soil their quarters, and confining the puppy to a limited area will encourage him to avoid making a mess. A young puppy must be taken out often, so watch your puppy closely and if he indicates he is about to relieve himself, take him outside at once. If he has an accident, scold him and take him out so he will associate the act of going outside with the need to relieve himself.

Always take the puppy out to relieve himself within an hour after meals. Take him to the same place each time, and make sure he relieves himself before you return him to the house. Restrict water for two hours before bedtime and take your puppy out just before you retire for the night. As soon as you (or he) wake in the morning, take him out again.

If you choose paper training, set aside a particular room and cover a large area of the floor with several thicknesses of newspapers. Each time the puppy relieves himself, remove the soiled papers and replace them with clean ones. As the puppy's control increases, gradually decrease the paper area, leaving part of the floor bare. If the puppy uses the bare floor, scold him mildly and put him on the papers, letting him know that that is where he is to relieve himself. As he understands the idea, increase the bare area until papers cover only space equal to approximately two full newspaper sheets. Allow him to continue using the papers, but begin taking him out on a leash at the times of day that he habitually relieves himself. Watch him closely when he is indoors and at the first sign that he needs to go, take him outdoors. Restrict his water for two hours before bedtime, but if necessary, permit him to use the papers before you retire for the night.

Puppy training pads are also available at your local pet supply. These waterproof pads are scented to attract the puppy and may accelerate the housebreaking process. They also protect carpeting or wood floors better than newspaper.

Using either method, the puppy will be housebroken in an amazingly short time. Once he has learned control he will need to relieve himself only four or five times a day.

BELGIANS AND OTHER ANIMALS

When introducing a new puppy or grown dog to another dog, always supervise their time together. Keep them separated when unattended until you are sure that one will not harm the other. A puppy has so much energy that it may get on the older dog's nerves after a time. Grown dogs new to each other should also be supervised when introduced to be sure that they will behave well together. Dogs establish a "pack order" or hierarchy, and may fight or behave aggressively until this is clearly established, whether there are two dogs or twelve. Never assume that because a puppy has a mild disposition around people, he will be submissive and not be challenged by another puppy or adult dog.

People sometimes ask whether there is a difference in temperament between males and females. Females are usually a little gentler than males, and more "homebodies." However, temperament in general is very similar between the sexes. You will find more difference in temperament between different bloodlines than between a male and a female.

Whether you should keep two or more dogs, or only one, should depend on how much your dog is a part of your household and family. If your Belgian is going to be mainly an outside dog and not spend much time with your family, then of course he would be happier to have a companion. If your Belgian is a real part of the family, he can be perfectly happy being the only dog. But, if you do acquire another Belgian, the two dogs can learn to get along quite well.

As for cats, if your puppy grows up with a cat it should not be a problem, but this also depends on the temperament of the cat and dog. If a puppy and

A well-mannered dog gets along with all creatures great and small. Primo and the Yorkie are good friends owned by Don and June Granander.

a grown cat play together, you need to be careful that the playful puppy does not get an eye scratched by a cat that prefers to be left alone. Introducing a grown dog to a cat can be a problem. You should plan for consistent, supervised training and use common sense.

Belgians have a natural instinct to herd, although it may be stronger in some dogs than others. They may decide to practice herding on any available animal, from ducks to cattle. If the animals belong to your neighbor, this may not be appreciated. If left to herd unsupervised,

Train your puppy to be well-mannered at all times. Chisom, owned by Pat Snow.

the Belgian will make up his own rules for herding (which could include chasing or biting) so proper training and fencing to keep your dog where he belongs is advisable.

BAD HABITS

Even after they have been well trained, dogs sometimes develop bad habits that are difficult to break. The best correction is prevention, starting with correcting or distracting the very young puppy. A puppy that is not allowed to develop bad behavior patterns will be far more pleasant to live with. However, in spite of your best efforts, you may need to correct some bad habits eventually.

Jumping on people is a common habit, and all members of the family must assist if it is to be broken. As the dog starts to jump up, take a step forward and raise your knee. As your knee strikes the dog's chest, command "Off!" in a scolding tone of voice. This takes the dog by surprise and he doesn't associate the discomfort with the person causing it. You must do this consistently, every time the dog jumps, and all members of the family must be instructed not to allow the behavior.

Occasionally a Belgian is too chummy with guests who don't care for dogs. If the dog has had obedience training, simply command "Come!" When he responds, have him sit beside you.

Persistent effort is needed to subdue a dog that barks without provocation. To correct this habit you must be close to the dog when he starts barking. Encircle his muzzle with both hands, hold his mouth shut, and command "Quiet!" in a firm voice. He should soon learn to respond. Then you can control his barking simply by giving the command. If this doesn't work or you cannot get close enough to put your hands on the dog when he is barking, try commanding "Quiet!" as you squirt him in the face with a water pistol.

Sniffing other dogs is another annoying habit. If your dog sniffs other dogs while he is off leash, ignoring your commands to come, he needs to review the lessons on basic behavior on leash. When the dog sniffs on leash, scold him, then pull him to you and walk away from the other dog. Praise when he walks past the other animal without trying to sniff.

A well-trained Belgian is a joy when you travel. No matter how well he responds, however, he should never be permitted off leash when you are walking in a strange area. Distractions are tempting, and there is always the chance that he might be attacked by other dogs. So whenever your dog travels with you, take his collar and leash along—and use them.

THE CANINE GOOD CITIZEN PROGRAM

The AKC has a Canine Good Citizen Certification which any dog, purebred or not, can earn. The test of your dog's manners and training to achieve this status is not a competition. You and your dog are not required to perform with precision. The purpose of the program is to ensure that your dog becomes a respected member of the community, and to encourage responsible pet ownership. Dogs that run loose and destroy neighbors' property are a nuisance and foster a hatred for dogs in general. A trained dog reflects favorably on its owner. Everyone benefits from this basic training.

The Canine Good Citizen course is a relaxed, fun program that you and your dog will enjoy. There are approximately ten simple categories in which the dog will be tested. Every dog must respond to at least four basic commands which are necessary if he is to be acceptable in public: "Heel," "Sit," "Down," and "Stay." You and your dog will work with others in public, as well as at home. Once your dog understands how to please you and learns what you expect of him, he will look forward to the training sessions as a special treat.

Many dog clubs, private obedience schools, kennels, and other organizations throughout the country offer classes to prepare your dog for Canine Good Citizen certification. Most of these organizations sponsor a Canine Good Citizen Test upon completion of the course. If a course is not available in your area, you and your dog can work with a booklet outlining the test rules and regulations which you can order from the AKC. I encourage you to seek certification for your dogs and join the ranks of thousands who have attained the Canine Good Citizen Certification.

Good manners are even more important with a group of dogs. The dam of this litter (lying in the front), Ch. Sherborne Mary Poppins, UDTX, Sch III, BH, FH, WH, owned and trained by Robert and Gail Brown, is shown with her famous grown-up litter. Left to right are Duquewood's Let It Rip, CDX, TDX, Sch III, FH, BH; Duquewood's Forward March, UDT, Sch III, BH, CGC; Duquewood's Direct Hit, CD, TDX, Sch III, FH, BH, WH, CGC; Ch. Duquewood's Fire When Ready, UDT, Sch III, BH, WH, CGC; and Duquewood's Dust 'Em, CDX. What more evidence could there be that intelligence and trainability are inherited traits?

Ch. Sandevel's Image in Black, CD, looks well groomed. Owner, Sandra E. King. Photo © Lloyd W. Olson.

CHAPTER SEVEN
Off to the Beauty Parlor

BELGIAN SHEEPDOGS ARE AMONG the easier breeds to groom. How much grooming your dog needs will depend on your regular grooming habits and on the terrain in which your dog spends most of his time. A house dog that runs on a well-kept lawn will require less time to groom than a dog that runs or works in weeds and high grass. Burrs, seeds, and grass become embedded in the coat, and the longer they are neglected the longer it takes to work them out without damaging the coat and causing discomfort to the dog. Foreign objects in the coat also can cause skin irritation and scratching, resulting in open lesions.

Start with short grooming sessions until your puppy becomes adjusted to the routine. After a few sessions he will look forward to the additional attention and to your personal touch.

THE COAT

Belgian Sheepdogs should have a medium-harsh, straight outer coat with a thick, dense undercoat which is necessary for extremes in weather. This double coat provides protection from the elements. The outer coat protects his body from rain and snow, while the undercoat provides insulation against heat or cold. Belgians usually shed their coat with the beginning of warm weather. The undercoat loosens gradually and must be removed to prevent matting and discomfort.

A short, daily brushing session will remove the loose hair. Brushing a Belgian is not a major project, unless you wait until an accumulation of dead hair has started to mat and tangle. Never trim or groom your Belgian in such a way that the coat gives the appearance of an open coat. Instead, the long outer coat should fall naturally to repel moisture and protect the undercoat. It should lie flat and follow the contour of the body.

EQUIPMENT

Grooming will be much easier and more enjoyable if you have the proper tools and either a grooming table with an adjustable arm for securing the dog's head or a crate with a grooming table top. Either rubber matting or carpeting will provide a non-slip surface. It is important to have a sturdy table or crate that will not wobble and create a sense of insecurity.

The tools are a matter of choice and also depend on the condition of the dog's coat. I prefer a wire brush with teeth about an inch long (called a pin brush), a good-quality natural-bristle brush, a comb with medium-spaced teeth, nail clippers, a nail file, a pair of surgical-type scissors with blunt points, and a pair of single-sided, fine-tooth thinning shears. You may also want a short, flat wire brush called a slicker brush for brushing the leg feathering, feet, and behind the ears.

GROOMING YOUR PUPPY

Short grooming sessions should begin while the puppy is still with his littermates. The breeder can begin by brushing the puppy with a soft bristle brush while he is standing or lying on the floor. A quiet, gentle tone of voice will help calm the puppy and give it a secure feeling. Start and end with a play session. Teach the puppy to lie on either side while you stroke and brush him. Accustom the puppy to having his feet held, then either clip or file the end of the nail to blunt it. This should be done weekly. If the puppy gets dirty, dampen his coat with a spray bottle and lukewarm water. Work the water into the coat and then use a soft towel to dry him. When you are finished, offer a little treat. This early handling gives the breeder insight into the temperament of each puppy, which will be of great value when it comes time to train them or time for them to go to a new owner.

Most puppies are afraid of heights and must be exposed gradually to being placed on a grooming table. Make sure the footing is secure and that the table does not wobble. A rubber mat is the best surface. In fact, if you don't have a table, place a rubber bath mat on a solid crate and use that for your grooming surface. You may need an assistant to hold the puppy at first.

Short sessions are the key. What your puppy does now will set the pattern for his behavior in the future when longer, more intense grooming sessions are needed

Between eight and ten weeks the puppy is in a critical period when it is easy to instill fear. All grooming at this age should be done gently and with the reassurance of a soothing voice. Try not to do anything that hurts the puppy. A bad experience at this age can stay with the puppy for the rest of his life, causing grooming to become a hassle.

A grooming arm and loop helps keep the dog in place while you groom. "Dazzle," Ch. La Neige Talk of the Town being brushed by owner Pat Snow.

A favorite toy and secure footing help this young puppy to get used to the grooming table. Note the slicker brush (left) and pin brush (right) lying on the table.

Keep sessions short and talk quietly to the puppy to help him feel secure.

GROOMING PROCEDURES

When you are ready to do a thorough job of grooming, place your dog on a grooming table or crate. Secure him to the grooming post with a noose, or have someone hold his head to prevent him from moving around. Every groomer has his or her own procedure, and it makes no difference as long as the result is satisfactory.

Brushing

Massage the body and skin with your fingers and stir up the hair. This will loosen dandruff caused by dryness and stimulate circulation and the secretion of the skin's natural oils. Brush

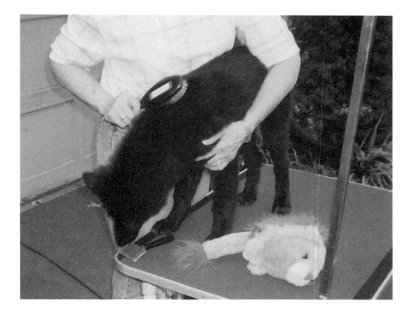

Always use a soft brush on a puppy and be gentle. Brush against the lay of the coat. "Abbey," owned by Pat Snow.

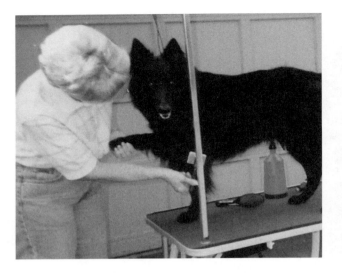
Brush the entire coat, including the leg fringe.

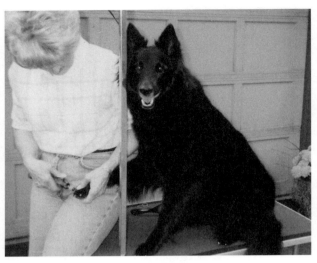
Snip a small amount from the tip of the toenails. Keep the show dog's nails short at all times to prevent the toes from splaying and the dog from slipping on cement.

"Dazzle," Ch. La Neige Talk of the Town, is misted with water by owner Pat Snow as a finishing touch before going to the show ring.

against the lay of the coat, from the rear toward the head, using a natural bristle brush. While doing this, check for fleas, ticks, or skin abrasions. Next, brush from the head towards the tail. This will loosen dead hair, which then can be removed with a comb or wire brush. When you have finished with the removal of dead hair, use the bristle brush to once again brush the coat forward toward the head. Let the dog shake himself and his hair should fall into place.

At a show, handlers often use a spray bottle of water to keep the coat looking full and fresh. Spritzing the coat with water and then back brushing it will make the coat stand out. Some handlers use a stiffening or conditioning product, but it's better to follow AKC rules and not take the chance of being disqualified in the ring, which has happened. Coat conditioners can be used between shows to enhance the color, shine and condition of the coat and then bathed out before a show. Adding Omega 3 and Omega 6 oil or other products especially for the coat, and keeping your dog clean and free of parasites will also enhance his coat. Show dogs should be kept out of the sun on hot days or in hot, dry climates as the Belgian's black coat easily can sunburn, fade, or become dry and split on the ends.

Trimming

The back of your dog's hocks may have excessive hair. Trim this off with thinning scissors. Using thinning shears will create a much neater appearance than what you get when using a straight scissors. The metatarsus, or what we commonly call the hock, should have a straight up-and-down, clean appearance.

Excess hair also grows on the back of the front pasterns. Remove this hair a short distance above the foot (up to the pad on the foreleg) using the thinning scissors. The fringe of hair on the upper front legs rarely needs trimming. Just brush out any mats or tangles with a slicker brush.

Belgians have a cat foot with arched toes. Trim around the foot to give a rounded appearance. Cut off excess hair around the outside of the feet and from between the pads using a curved scissors or thinning shears. Excess hair around the pads on the bottom of the foot and between the toes can collect grass and seeds in summer and snow and ice in winter, and cause irritation and soreness. Next pull any excess hair between the pads upward between the toes to the top of the foot with your fingers. Remove these tufts of hair with a small, blunt-nose scissors.

Sometimes hair along the loin area will grow in different lengths and detract from the contour of the body. Trim this hair with thinning scissors to create a more even look. Never cut a straight line across the stomach area. Follow the lines of the body and just trim a small amount from the tips of the hairs.

Trimming the whiskers of a show dog is a matter of choice. Most exhibitors do trim the whiskers to give a cleaner look to the muzzle, and also even up the hair around the lip line. If you do not intend to show your dog, this is not necessary.

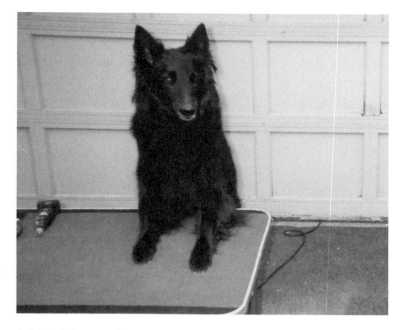

Adult Belgians readily learn to jump on the grooming table, but be careful about letting them jump off. Landing on hard surfaces or slipping as they land has caused injury to many show dogs. In order to hasten drying time before a show, many exhibitors use a blow dryer. The hose to a livestock-type dryer can be seen beneath the grooming table. If you show a lot, a blower is an excellent investment. Not only does it dry—it also removes loose hair, fluffs out the undercoat, and can be used as a substitute for brushing during touch-ups. Blow the coat against the lay of the coat from the roots outward. Let the dog shake himself to flatten and smooth the coat afterward.

Make sure there are no mats in the coat just behind the ears or under the elbows. These areas are the easiest ones to get matted or to collect burrs or stickers. Check your dog's ears and teeth to make sure they are clean.

If you are preparing to show your Belgian, do all trimming except for the whiskers at least a week before a show. You can do a light touch-up the day before the show if necessary, but be careful not to remove too much hair at that time, giving your dog an artificial appearance. Trimming should not be obvious to the judge or those at ringside. The object of trimming is to create a neat, clean outline.

Toenails

Unless your dog is very active or is kept on a hard surface like cement, his toenails will need regular trimming every one to two weeks. Long toenails cause an unnatural stance that can in turn cause lameness and splayed toes. Splayed feet affect the gait and impair the dog's ability to move correctly.

Belgians have black toes and it is hard to see the blood vein line. Take care not to cut into the quick as this is very painful for the dog and can cause heavy bleeding. Nevertheless, always keep a preparation such as Quik Stop handy just in case you accidentally cut too deep. Snip a small amount from the tip of the nail to avoid cutting the blood vessels in the nail, and then file the tip. Draw the file in only one direction. A downward stroke will give a more finished look.

Do not overlook the dewclaws on the front legs. They curl under as they grow, sometimes circling back and piercing the skin. Some breeders remove dewclaws when the puppies are young. If they have not been removed, include them in your weekly care of the nails.

If your dog's nails get too long, it may be easier to take him to your veterinarian or groomer and have her trim them. Once the nails are cut back, a few strokes with a file every week should keep them at a proper length.

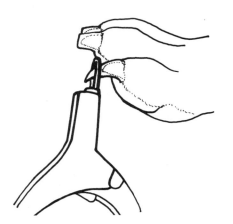

Trimming the nail.

Eyes, Ears, and Teeth

Mucus can collect in the corners of your dog's eyes. Wipe the eyes with a piece of cotton or soft tissue, being careful not to touch the eyeball and cause irritation. If there is a definite discharge, you should check with your veterinarian. If there is any redness in the eye, you can use an ophthalmic ointment or moisture drops to soothe and clear the eye. If redness continues, it may be the result of a foreign object in the eye, in which case the eye needs to be flushed. Some people use a mild boric acid solution for this.

Check your dog's ears often. You can remove dirt and wax from the folds of the upper ear with a swab dipped in a mild solution of boric acid, or you can wrap some cotton dampened with witch hazel around your forefinger. There are many commercial ear cleaners on the market as well. Clean only that part of the inner ear that you can see. Do not probe in the ear canal. If your dog constantly shakes his head, or twitches or scratches at his ear, a seed or some other foreign object may be embedded in the ear canal. If this is the case, it must be removed by a veterinarian. Internal ear canker can cause the same symptoms. Ear mites are another problem that can cause great discomfort to a dog. In all cases of ear disease, your veterinarian's services should be obtained at once, for a delay may result in a chronic, and sometimes incurable, condition.

Cleaning a dog's teeth can be a problem if the dog is not introduced to the procedure at an early age. Most dogs resist examination of the teeth. The dog in his natural state kept his teeth in good condition, but through years of domesticity, dogs, like ourselves, suffer from tooth decay and tartar deposits. Tartar accumulates when a dog eats soft food over a long period of time. If it accumulates in large quantities, it pushes back the gums, exposing the roots of the teeth, which then become loosened. Decomposed foods become lodged in the cavities, the result being that pyorrhea may develop, along with irritation. Unless older dogs have proper tooth care, abscesses can occur at the base of the root system.

Occasionally giving the dog a large knucklebone that will not splinter may help keep tartar from accumulating. Hard dog biscuits are good for the teeth as well as being a pleasant treat. A number of companies now make dog bones that are especially formulated to reduce tartar. While these products are not sufficient on their own to keep your dog's teeth clean, they can supplement a regular cleaning regimen.

If a large quantity of tartar accumulates on your dog's teeth, have your dog anesthetized and let your vet do the cleaning. Bad teeth and infected gums contribute to a host of other problems, including heart trouble, in older dogs. An ounce of prevention is worth a pound of cure, so start early and don't neglect your Belgian's teeth.

BATHING

A normal, healthy dog does not require frequent bathing. A Belgian Sheepdog's skin is rich in oil glands and deficient in sweat glands. The natural oils prevent the skin from becoming dry and help keep the coat water-resistant. If you bathe the dog too often, this natural oil is removed and the skin can become irritated. The dog may scratch and bite himself, even to the point of causing open abrasions which are slow to heal.

A well-groomed Belgian will not have a doggy odor. Your dog will have to have a bath if he has been in mud or has rolled in some offensive substance that cannot be removed with a brush. If you do not have a kennel room and tub, you can put a non-slip mat in your bathtub. To avoid getting the floor wet, spread newspaper on the floor in front of the tub. Plug the dog's ears with cotton to prevent water from getting into the ear canal. To protect the eyes, some people use a drop of ophthalmic ointment, which is soothing as well as protective. There are numerous soaps and shampoos on the market, and they all have their good and bad qualities. Some of these soaps contain carbolic acid and bichloride of mercury. These soaps, though they kill fleas, sometimes cause eczema, which is quite difficult to cure. A mild shampoo, even human baby shampoo, will do a good job.

Bath water should be tepid—never too hot or too cold. Work the shampoo well into the coat and then rinse every trace of it from the coat. Wash your dog's head last, using a washcloth to avoid getting shampoo in the dog's eyes.

When a dog comes out of a bath he will shake himself, and that is when you get an extra bath if you are not careful. Drop a large towel over his back and let him shake the excess water from his coat; then rub him vigorously until he is dry. If the weather is warm, you can put him outside on the grass to finish drying, but if it is cold keep him inside until he is thoroughly dry. In hot weather you can put a drop cloth on the ground and bathe your dog outside using your garden hose. It works just as well and saves a lot of work cleaning up after an indoor bath.

If you are going to show your dog, bathe your Belgian a few days before the show to allow time for the natural oils to return to the coat. Brushing will help restore the oil and give the coat a nice sheen.

BIS Ch. La Neige's Charming Duchess, breeder/owners Patricia and H. E. Snow. Shown by James Moses. Photo © Bishop Photography.

CHAPTER EIGHT

In the Limelight

DOG SHOWS PROVIDE A VENUE where you can test the success of your breeding program or see how your dog compares with other specimens of his breed. Dogs compete for points toward a championship as well as class, group, and Best in Show awards. There are classes for all ages of dogs as well as handling classes for junior handlers. Obedience and other performance classes may also be held in conjunction with the dog show. For hundreds of thousands of dog fanciers, dog shows provide an absorbing hobby.

The idea of comparing breeding stock began centuries ago. It was common practice to hold agricultural fairs in conjunction with spring and fall religious festivals, and to these gatherings, cattle, dogs, and other livestock were brought for exchange. As time went on, it became customary to provide entertainment, too. Dogs often participated in such sporting events as bull baiting, bear baiting, and ratting. The dog that exhibited the greatest skill in the arena was also the one that brought the highest price when the time came for barter or sale. These fairs were the forerunners of modern dog shows and, although they seem a far cry from our highly organized bench shows and field trials, they played an important role in shaping the development of purebred dogs.

The first organized dog show was held at Newcastle, England, in 1859. Later that same year, a show was held at Birmingham. At both shows dogs were divided into four classes and only Pointers and Setters were entered. In 1860, the first dog show in Germany was held at Apoldo, where nearly one hundred dogs were exhibited and entries were divided into six groups. Interest expanded rapidly, and by the time the Paris Exhibition was held in 1878, the dog show was a fixture of international importance.

SHOWING IN THE USA

In the United States, the first organized bench show was held in 1874 in conjunction with the meeting of the Illinois Sportsmen's Association in Chicago, and all entries were dogs of sporting breeds. Although the show was a rather casual affair, interest spread quickly to Oswego, New York; Mineola, Long Island; and Memphis, Tennessee. The latter combined a bench show with the first organized field trial in the United States. In January 1875, the first all-breed show in the United States was held in Detroit, Michigan. After that, interest increased rapidly, but rules were not always uniform. There was no organization to coordinate activities until the American Kennel Club was founded in September 1884.

Now the largest dog-registering organization in the world, the AKC is an association of several hundred member clubs—all breed, specialty, field trial, and obedience groups—each represented by a delegate. The several thousand shows and trials held annually in the United States do much to stimulate interest in breeding to produce better looking and more sound purebred dogs. AKC shows provide a means for breeders to measure the merits of their work as compared with accomplishments of other breeders.

Show Competition

At conformation shows, dogs are rated comparatively on their physical qualities (or conformation) in accordance with breed Standards which have been approved by the American Kennel Club. Characteristics such as size, coat, color, placement of eye or ear, general soundness, and structure are the basis of selecting the best dog in a class. Only purebred dogs are eligible to compete, and if the show is one where points toward championship are to be awarded, a dog must be at least six months old.

There are various types of conformation shows. An all-breed show has classes for all of the breeds recognized by the American Kennel Club as well as a Miscellaneous Class for breeds not yet recognized. A sanctioned match is an informal meeting where dogs compete, but not for championship points. A specialty show is confined to a single breed. Other shows may restrict entries to champions of record, to American-bred dogs, etc. Competition for Junior Championship or for Best Brace, Best Team, or Best Local Dog may be included. Obedience and sometimes Agility competitions are held in conjunction with many bench shows.

Conformation shows may be either "benched" or "unbenched." At the former, each dog is assigned an individual numbered stall where he must remain throughout the show except for times when he is being judged, groomed, or exercised. At unbenched shows, no stalls are provided and dogs are kept in their owner's cars or in crates when not being judged.

A conformation show actually constitutes an elimination contest. To begin with, the dogs of a single breed compete with others of their breed in one of the regular classes: Puppy, 12 to 18 Month-Old, Novice, Bred by Exhibitor, American-Bred, or Open, and finally, Winners, where the top dogs of the preceding five classes are judged for Winners Dog and Winners Bitch.

When the Winners Class is divided by sex, championship points are awarded the Winners Dog and Winners Bitch. If the Winners Class is not divided by sex, championship points are awarded the dog or bitch named Winners. The number of points awarded varies, depending upon such factors as the number of dogs competing, the Schedule of Points established by the Board of Directors of the AKC, and whether the dog goes on to win Best of Breed, Group, or Best in Show.

In order to become a champion, a dog must win fifteen points, including

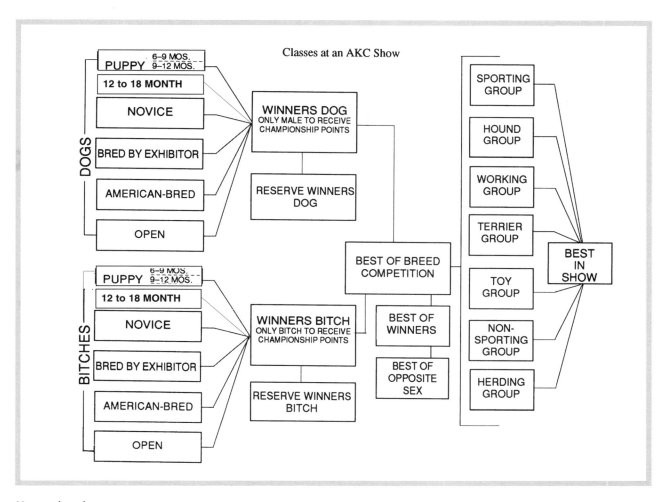

How a dog show progresses.

points from at least two major wins—that is, at least two shows where three or more points are awarded. The major wins must be under two different judges, and one or more of the remaining points must be won under a third judge. The most points ever awarded at a show is five and the least is one; so, in order to become a champion, a dog must be exhibited and win in at least three shows. Most dogs are shown many times before earning a championship.

The next step is the judging for Best of Breed (or Best of Variety of Breed). Here the Winners Dog and Winners Bitch (or the dog named Winners if only one prize is awarded) compete with any champions that are entered, together with any undefeated dogs that have competed in additional non-regular classes. One of the dogs is chosen Best of Breed (or Best of Variety of Breed), and a dog of the opposite sex is chosen as Best of Opposite Sex. The judge also awards Best of Winners to the Winners Dog or Winners Bitch.

The dog named Best of Breed (or Best of Variety of Breed) then goes on to compete with the other Best of Breed winners in his Group. There are seven different Groups. The dogs that win each Group competition then compete for the final and highest honor, Best in Show.

Two Best of Breed winning Belgians. Top, Ch. Bel-Reve's Pistolero (Photo © J. Ashbey) and bottom, Ch. Bel-Reve's Richmond, who has multiple group placements (Photo © Cott). Both dogs bred and owned by Bill and Cathy Daugherty. Note how the handlers' light colored clothing sets off the outline of the dogs.

The *AKC Gazette*, published by the American Kennel Club, and other dog magazines contain lists of forthcoming shows together with names and addresses of sponsoring organizations to which you may write for entry forms and information relative to fees and closing dates. Before entering your dog in a show for the first time, you should familiarize yourself with the regulations and rules governing competition. You may secure such information from The American Kennel Club or from a local dog club. It is essential that you also learn the AKC-approved Standard for your breed so you will be fully aware of characteristics worthy of merit as well as those considered faulty or possibly even serious enough to disqualify the dog from competition. For instance, monorchidism (failure of one testicle to descend) and cryptorchidism (failure of both testicles to descend) are disqualifying faults in all breeds.

SHOWING YOUR BELGIAN

Showing a Belgian Sheepdog is easy. I think that this is why so many Belgian owners show their own dogs. However, professional handlers are more common today than in the past, because the breed has become widely recognized and has taken its rightful place in Group and Best in Show wins.

Basic training, which may be more intense later, includes learning to be calm and steady when examined by persons other than the owner. The handler needs practice as well, so he or she does not get nervous and pass this on to the dog in the show ring. You will need to learn how to position or "stack" your dog, how to get his attention for the judge, how to execute the ring patterns

This six-month-old pup is practicing "baiting" or watching the handler intently. This is important when showing. Ch. Bel-Reve's Sahara Wind, owned by Ann Boles and Cathy Daugherty.

smoothly and correctly, and to understand the judge's directions while you are in the ring. Many clubs and training centers offer classes or practice sessions to help you prepare for conformation classes. Go to them. You will find them invaluable and they will save you many a wasted entry fee.

The overall picture of the Belgian Sheepdog is a square, medium-size dog with well-set, triangular ears and dark, expressive eyes. The body lines fit together in an elegant outline that gives the general appearance of squareness, strength, and solidarity, with an extremely proud carriage of the head and neck. The collarette adorning the neck frames the face and ears and adds grace to the arch of the neck.

The Belgian's motion during gaiting should be smooth, light, and easy.

A puppy getting some early training and socialization at a match. Here, the handler is teaching him to set himself up and stand quietly.

Correctly posed and alert for the judge, this dog exhibits the correct square appearance. Ch. Lorjen Heir Apparent, CD, owned by Maxine and Roger Ellis.

Note the extension and angulation of this Belgian. Ch. Zachariah Coburg of Van Mell, CDX, was Best of Breed at the 1976 BSCA National Specialty show. Owners, John and Darlene Eaton.

Belgian Sheepdogs single track at a fast gait. They do not have hard-driving action. Give the Belgian a loose lead and match your own stride to his. Never string up the head of your dog with a tight, restraining lead. It will throw off his smooth, effortless gait.

Keep in mind that you want to give the impression of a square dog when your Belgian Sheepdog is standing posed, or "stacked," for the judge. All four legs should be squarely under the dog. He should exhibit proper placement and angulation in both the front and rear assemblies. Whatever you do, don't hassle your dog by placing his feet if they are not perfect. Do your training at home, not in the show ring. Relax and enjoy yourself while in the ring; there will be other dog shows to win another time and place. Fussing with your dog will only serve to call attention to any flaws you are trying to correct, and will make your dog dislike the show ring.

If possible, you should first attend a show as a spectator and observe judging procedures from ringside. Joining a local breed club and participating in sanctioned matches before entering an all-breed show is also helpful. Go to as many match shows as you can before entering a regular show. Ask questions from the other exhibitors after they have finished showing. Most breeders like to talk about their dogs when they have time, but not when they are getting ready to go into the ring.

AT THE SHOW

Pack for the show the day before so you don't have to rush. Classes generally run from 8:00 A.M. until 2:00 or 3:00 P.M., after which the group judging will begin. Plan to arrive a couple of hours before your class so your dog can get used to the noise and confusion. Food and water dishes will be needed, as well as a supply of the food and water to which the dog is accustomed. Brushes and combs are also necessary, so that you can give the dog's coat a final grooming after you arrive at the show.

Familiarize yourself with the schedule of classes ahead of time, for the dog must be fed and exercised and permitted to relieve himself, and any last-minute grooming completed before his class is called. Talk to your dog and reassure him. This will give him confidence in himself. Remember, no one is judging *you*, they are looking at your pretty dog

Before your class, walk over and watch the pattern the judge is using; you will be better prepared to respond to his instructions. It saves time and you will have more confidence in what you need to do to show your dog to the best advantage.

Make sure that your dog is clean and well brushed. You should be properly dressed as well. Your personal appearance should exude confidence and professionalism. Women generally wear long, slender skirts or slacks that will not flop in the dog's face. Men often wear a suit and tie or a sport jacket. Choose a color that compliments your dog. Never wear a black outfit when showing a Belgian Sheepdog. The judge will be unable to see your dog's outline or gait any time you are positioned behind the dog.

The dog should be equipped with a show lead and a show collar—never an

A lightweight chain collar is sometimes used as a show collar. It should be just long enough to slide comfortably over the dog's head and should be worked down into the coat at the top of his neck. Attach a lightweight show lead.

A martingale-type show lead is another possible choice. These collars are constructed out of nylon or leather.

ornamented or spiked collar. There are several types: narrow leather collars and leads, a small, dressy chain

For benched shows, either a bench crate or a metal-link bench chain to fasten the dog to the bench will be needed. For unbenched shows, the dog's crate should be taken along so that he may be confined in comfort when he is not appearing in the ring. A dog should never be left in a car with all the windows closed. In hot weather the temperature can become unbearable in a very short time. Heat exhaustion and even death can result from even a short period of confinement in a vehicle.

Both you and the dog should be ready to enter the ring unhurriedly. A good deal of skill in conditioning, training, and handling is required if a dog is

RING PATTERNS

During the individual examination of your dog, the judge will instruct you to move in one of the following four patterns. Watch the class ahead of you to see which one the judge is requesting on that particular day. You should practice these patterns at home or in a class until your dog will move at a smooth trot in a straight line and turn smoothly on command. With most breeds it is preferable to have the dog moving on a loose lead. If the lead is too tight it will throw off the dog's gait. As you return to the judge, your dog should stop smoothly about six feet in front of the judge and give you his alert, focused attention. This shows his expression and lack of fear of strangers. Teach your dog to stop squarely, stand, and bait while the judge gets one last overall impression. Then, on the judge's signal, take your dog around the ring to the right and back to the end of the lineup.

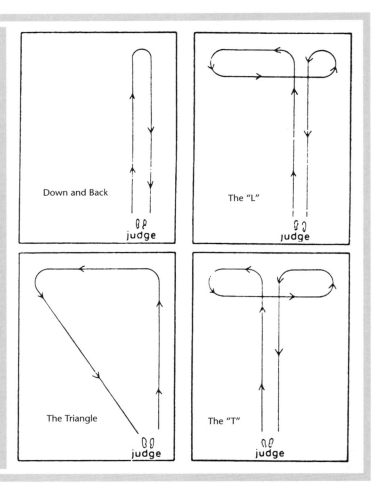

to be presented properly. And it is essential that the handler himself be composed, for a jittery handler will transmit his nervousness to his dog.

Once the class is assembled in the ring, the judge will ask that the dogs be paraded in line, moving counterclockwise in a circle. If you have trained your dog well, you will have no difficulty controlling him in the ring. He must change pace quickly and gracefully, and walk and trot elegantly and proudly with his head erect. The show dog must also stand quietly for inspection, posing like a statue for several minutes while the judge observes his outline in detail and examines his teeth, feet, coat, and structure. When the judge calls your dog forward for individual inspection, do not attempt to converse, but do answer any questions he may ask.

The first ribbon that you and your dog win all by yourselves will be the prettiest and the most special ribbon you will ever win. Soon you will be looking for an entry blank for another show.

FROM THE JUDGE'S POINT OF VIEW

As a judge, I do not want to walk up to dogs that don't even know I'm there and that could react negatively to someone coming up to examine them. The dogs can be alert and interested in the bait, but should not be so intent that they are not aware of the judge's approach.

Am. Can. BISS Ch. Sumer Wynd's Dana of Isengard, HX, CDX, TD, MX, MXJ, HOF, WDC-X, WD-H owner Lorra Miller and breeder Dennette Cockley. Photo © Chuck and Sandy Tatham.

The judge should look for these qualities and behaviors: overall balance, alertness, personality, standing quietly while the judge examines them for bone structure, moving smoothly with their handler, maintaining the pace set by the handler rather than lagging or forging, showing correct movement and correct type according to the breed Standard.

As the judge examines the class, he measures each dog against the ideal described in the Standard, then measures the dogs against each other in a comparative sense and selects for first place the dog that comes closest to conforming to the Standard for his breed.

If your dog isn't among the winners, don't grumble. If he places first, don't brag, for a bad loser is disgusting, but a poor winner is insufferable. There is always another show and another day.

Am. Can. Ch. La Neige's Charming Duchess breeder/owners Patricia and H. E. Snow. Photo © Alverson.

Agility is one of the most popular dog sports. Photo © Judith Strom.

CHAPTER NINE

Talent Shows

OBEDIENCE COMPETITION

For hundreds of years, dogs were used in England and Germany for police and guard work and their working potential was evaluated through tests devised to show agility, strength, and courage. Organized training was also popular with English and German breeders, although at first it was practiced primarily for the purpose of training large breeds in aggressive tactics.

There was little interest in obedience training in the United States until 1933 when Mrs. Whitehouse Walker returned from England and enthusiastically introduced the sport. Two years later Mrs. Walker persuaded the American Kennel Club to approve organized obedience activities and to assume jurisdiction over obedience rules. Since then interest has increased at a phenomenal rate. Obedience competition is not only a sport the average spectator can follow readily, but also a sport for which the average owner easily can train his own dog.

Obedience competition is suitable for all breeds. Furthermore, there is no limit to the number of dogs that win in competition, for each dog is scored individually on the basis of a point rating system. The dog is judged on his response to certain commands, and if he gains a high enough score in three successive trials under different judges, he wins an obedience title.

The qualifying score is a minimum of 170 points out of a possible total of 200, with no score in any one exercise less than 50 percent of the points allotted for that exercise. Since the titles are progressive from CD through UDX, earlier titles are dropped as a dog acquires the next higher title. After they achieve the Utility Dog title, dogs can continue to compete and accumulate points toward an Obedience Championship. To be eligible for this title, a dog must have earned the Utility Dog title and then must earn an additional one hundred championship points in certain types of competition, placing first three times under different judges.

Trials for obedience trained dogs are held separately as well as in conjunction with large conformation shows. Obedience training clubs are active in almost

OBEDIENCE TITLES AWARDED

CD—Companion Dog
CDX—Companion Dog Excellent
UD—Utility Dog
UDX—Utility Dog Excellent
OTCH—Obedience Trial Champion

Retrieve over the high jump. Photo © Christine McHenry, Skipper Productions.

all communities. Information concerning forthcoming trials and lists of obedience training clubs are included regularly in the *AKC Gazette* and other dog magazines. Pamphlets containing rules and regulations governing obedience competition are available upon request from the American Kennel Club. Rules are revised occasionally, so if you are interested in participating in obedience competition, you should be sure your copy of the regulations is current.

Preparation and Training

An ideal way to train a dog for obedience competition is to join an obedience class or a training club. In organized class work, beginners' classes cover basic heeling, sit and down stays, and the "come" command. Through class work you will develop greater precision than is possible when training your dog by yourself. Amateur handlers often cause the dog to be penalized. If the handler fails to abide by the rules, it is the dog that suffers the penalty. A common infraction is using more than one signal or command where regulations stipulate only one may be used. Class work will help eliminate such errors, which the owner may make unconsciously if he is working alone. Working with a class will also acquaint both dog and handler with ring procedure so that obedience trials will not present unforeseen problems.

Thirty or more owners and dogs often comprise a class, and exercises are performed in unison, with individual instruction provided if it is required. The procedures followed in training—in fact, even wording of various commands—may vary from instructor to instructor. Equipment used will vary somewhat, also, but will usually include a training collar and leash, a long line, a dumbbell, and a jumping stick. The latter may be a short length of heavy doweling or a broom handle, and both it and the dumbbell are usually painted white for increased visibility.

Most beginning classes will not fully prepare you and your dog for competition. A second Novice obedience class may be needed. When you finish that class you may want to take your dog to trials and compete in Novice obedience before deciding whether to continue training, or you can proceed right on through the next level, the Open class, while you work on getting his Companion Dog title.

A bitch in season must never be taken to a training class, so before enrolling a female dog you should determine whether she may be expected to come into season before classes are scheduled to end. If you think she will, it is better to wait and enroll her in a later course, rather than to start the course and then miss classes for several weeks.

In addition to the time devoted to actual work in class, the dog must have regular, daily practice sessions at home. Exercise the dog before each class or home training session so he will not be highly excited when the session starts, and he must be given an opportunity to relieve himself before the session begins. (Should he have an accident during the class, it is your responsibility to clean up after him.) The dog should be fed several hours before the class begins or after the class is over—never just before a training session.

Obedience Trials

As with conformation competition, the best place to start is to enter a small, informal "match" show the first time. The obedience classes may be held just like at an AKC Obedience Trial, or they may be what are called "show and go" classes, which means you come and enter, show your dog and leave without waiting as long as you would at a regular match. It is important to plan to arrive early for most obedience competitions because the novice classes tend to be held first thing in the morning.

In addition to collar, leash, and other equipment, you should take your dog's food and water pans and a supply of the food and water to which he is accustomed. You should also take his brushes and combs in order to give him a last-minute brushing before you enter

This Belgian is executing the "come" exercise off lead.

Walking or jogging with your dog can provide companionship as well as protection. Kaye Hall does a "fast-forward" heeling exercise with "Jean Jean", Ch. Belle Noire Laxson du Jet.

The obedience down-stay exercise.

A team of Belgians heel on leash. Photos © Judith Strom.

"I'm ready to go!" Zula V. Siegestor, UDX, TT, CGC, owned by Marion Egly.

the ring. It is important that the dog look his best even though he will not be judged on his appearance.

Dogs are usually called in the order in which their names appear in the catalog, so as soon as you arrive at the show, acquaint yourself with the schedule. If your dog is not the first to be judged, spend some time at ringside observing the routine so you will know what to expect when your turn comes.

Exercise your dog, permit him to relieve himself, and give him a drink of water before your class. Once your dog enters the ring, be sure to give voice commands distinctly so he will hear and understand. There will be many distractions at ringside.

The Novice class is for dogs that have not won the title Companion Dog. In Novice A, no person who has previously handled a dog that has won a CD title in the obedience ring at a licensed or member trial, and no person who has regularly trained such a dog, may enter. The handler must be the dog's owner or a member of the owner's immediate family. In Novice B, dogs may be handled by the owner or any other person. Novice competition includes such exercises as heeling on and off lead, the stand for examination, coming on recall, and the long sit and the long down.

The Open A class is for dogs that have won the CD title but have not won the CDX title. Obedience judges and licensed handlers may not enter or handle dogs in this class. Each dog must be handled by the owner or by a member of the owner's immediate family. **The Open B class** is for dogs that have won the title CD or CDX. A dog may continue to compete in this class after it has won the UD title. Dogs in this class may be handled by the owner or any other person. In Open competition, the dog must perform such exercises as heeling free, the drop on recall, and the retrieve on the flat and over the high jump. Also, he must execute the broad jump and the long sit and long down.

The Utility class is for dogs that have won the title CDX, and dogs that have already earned the title UD may continue to compete as well. Dogs may be handled by the owner or any other person. Provided the AKC approves, a club may choose to divide the Utility class into Utility A and Utility B. When this is done, the Utility A class is for dogs that have won the title CDX and have not won the title UD. Obedience judges and licensed handlers may not enter or handle dogs in this class. All other dogs that are eligible for the Utility class but not eligible for Utility A may be entered in Utility B. In the Utility class, competition includes scent discrimination, the directed retrieve, the signal exercise, directed jumping, and the group examination.

The qualifying score for each class is a minimum of 170 points out of a possible total of 200, with no score in any one exercise less than 50 percent of the points allotted. Since the CD and UD titles are progressive, earlier titles are dropped as a dog acquires the next higher title.

TRACKING TESTS

When a dog tracks, he is following the scent left by a person who traveled through an area. According to William Syrotuck in his book, *Scent and the Scenting Dog,* the average dog has about over one hundred million olfactory cells, while man has only about five million. When a person travels across an area, small particles of skin and dust fall on the ground and vegetation, as well as linger in the air. It is truly amazing to watch a dog find and follow this trail.

The sport of tracking has drawn an increasing number of dedicated trainers in recent years, partly because is an active, outdoor activity that high energy dogs like the Belgian Sheepdog enjoy,

Ch. Grand Fond Amazone Noire , CD, TD, running at track at the Tulsa National Specialty. Owner, Kaye Hall.

Ch. Grand Fond Duc du Vignoble, UDTX, TT, CGC, HIT, AG, Select, is shown tracking in open country with his owner, Kaye Hall.

and partly because of the growing recognition of the value of search and rescue dogs, which begin their training with learning to track.

Tracking tests, like obedience trials, allow the dog to earn titles based on a performance score. These tests simulate finding articles left by a lost person. A tracklayer carrying personal articles such as a wallet or glove, walks along a course designated by the judge and drops the articles. The dog must then track where

TRACKING TITLES

TD—Tracking Dog
TDX—Tracking Dog Excellent
VST—Variable Surface Tracking
CT—Champion Tracker

the person walked and find the articles. Each level of test progresses in length and degree of difficulty.

Tracking tests are always held outdoors and, for obvious reasons, cannot be held at a dog show. Because there are relatively few tests held throughout the country and each test can only accommodate a few dogs, your entry is drawn from a pool and you may have to wait a long time to get in. Before you can enter, an AKC-approved judge must watch your dog run a track and issue a certification saying that your dog is truly ready.

There are three levels of noncompetitive tests: Tracking Dog (TD), Tracking Dog Excellent (TDX), and Versatile Surface Tracking (VST). The dog must follow a scent trail that is about a quarter mile in length and he must do it one-half to two hours after the scent is laid. He is required to find the scent object left by the tracklayer.

A dog that has earned all three tracking titles, TD, TDX, and VST, may use the title CT or Champion Tracker preceding his name.

SEARCH AND RESCUE

Search and rescue training takes tracking a step further and teaches the dog to find a lost person, dead or alive. This is not a competitive sport, but real service work. Search and rescue requires an agile, mentally solid and physically fit dog and handler. It is not for everyone. However, if you are interested in contributing a vital service to humanity, search and rescue or avalanche rescue work can be tremendously rewarding. Contact the National Association for Search and Rescue or ask your local tracking trainer about classes and opportunities in your area.

AGILITY

Agility is the fastest growing dog sport in America. Not only is it fun to compete in agility competition but it is also an exciting spectator sport. Agility is based on stadium horse jumping competition, and incorporates a variety of obstacles in a timed course that dog and handler must complete. It takes an agile, physically fit dog with sound temperament to perform on the many difficult

---

OTHER TITLES

HC—Herding Champion
DC—Dual Champion (Champion of Record (Ch.)
plus Herding Champion (HC))
TC—Triple Champion (Dual Champion (DC)
plus Obedience Trial Champion)
CGC—Canine Good Citizen
TDI—Therapy Dog International

Talent Shows

Photos © Christine McHenry, Skipper Productions.

AKC AGILITY TITLES

NA—Novice Agility
NAJ—Novice Jumper with Weaves
OA—Open Agility
OAJ—Open Jumper with Weaves
AX—Agility Excellent
AXJ—Excellent
JWW—Jumper with Weaves
MX—Master Agility Excellent
MXJ—Master Excellent Jumper with Weaves
MACH—Master Agility Champion

Chieho's Zarco Von Jet navigates a closed tunnel. Handler, Cindy Jaye.

and challenging obstacles in record time. Both trainer and dog have to be mentally alert to compete while disregarding all the applause and cheers of the audience during their performance. However, it is a competition that almost any reasonably active person can do well in, and it is both challenging and relaxing for your dog. Belgian Sheepdogs can easily excel in this sport.

The AKC booklet *Regulations for Agility Trials* lists the amount of obstacles that must be used, plus additional rules. The Novice class requires a minimum of twelve and a maximum of thirteen obstacles; Open class requires fifteen to seventeen; and the Excellent class, eighteen to twenty obstacles.

Dogs are timed from the start to finish line. The maximum attainable score in any class is 100 points. In order to earn a qualifying score, a dog must pass with a score of 85 points or better, and not receive any non-qualifying deduction. The dog must have a qualifying score to be eligible for a placement. Dogs that are successful can earn Agility titles.

In order to acquire an agility title, a dog must earn a qualifying score in his respective class on three separate occasions under two different judges. The AKC will identify dogs qualifying for titles by the appropriate title designation (NA, OA, AX, MX) following their registered names in all official AKC records. In each case, the higher title will supersede the preceding title.

In order to acquire the Master Agility Excellent title, a dog must acquire the Agility Excellent title and earn qualifying scores in the Excellent class at ten licensed or member agility trials. Credit toward the Agility Excellent title cannot be earned at the trial where the dog acquires the title. The Jumper With Weaves titles are earned in the same manner.

To obtain the Master Agility Champion (MACH) title, a dog must exhibit speed and consistency on the agility course. He must achieve a minimum of 750 championship points and 20 double qualifying scores from the Excellent B Standard Agility class and the Excellent B Jumpers with Weaves class. The initials "MACH" will be followed by a numeric designation indicating the number of times the dog has met the requirements for the title.

Chieho's Zarco Von Jet, handled by Cindy Jaye, scaling the A-frame.

Chieho's Zarco Von Jet exiting an open tunnel.

Belgian Sheepdog on an agility dog walk. Photo © Judith Strom.

Chieho's Zarco Von Jet shown jumping through an enclosed jump (now changed to a tire jump).

In addition to the AKC Agility trials, several other organizations also offer agility competitions and titles. Check with each organization for specific rules and regulations and a list of the titles that can be earned through that particular organization.

If you are interested in training your dog in Agility, you need to join an agility club or an obedience club which has the equipment. Rules change from time to time, so be sure to check with the appropriate organization for the latest version.

VERSATILITY CHAMPIONSHIP

If your Belgian earns an OTCH in Obedience, a CT in Tracking, and a MACH in Agility, he or she will be awarded the Versatile Companion Champion (VCCH) title as well.

SCHUTZHUND

Schutzhund means "protection dog" in German, and was developed as a test of the character and working ability of police dogs. The exercises required to earn Schutzhund titles are in three segments: tracking, obedience, and protection work. Again, this is not a sport for everyone, but if you do want to continue with advanced training, you will probably find other Belgian Sheepdog owners involved in a Schutzhund club near you because the breed is popular in this sport.

Several organizations in the United States offer Schutzhund trials and award titles, including the North American Working Dog Association and the United Schutzhund Clubs of America. The requirements of all the organizations are similar. The dog must earn at least seventy out of one hundred points in obedience and tracking, and at least eight points in protection at all levels of work. They must also pass all segments. The dog must be fourteen months or older and must pass a temperament test before he can enter Schutzhund competition. Training is offered only to members of a Schutzhund club or organization.

Schutzhund I

Schutzhund I is the first level for a protection-trained dog.

In the Tracking section, the dog must follow an unmarked track while on a twenty-foot lead. The track must be at least twenty minutes old and have two turns. The track is laid by the dog's own handler. Two articles are dropped which the dog must locate.

The Obedience section includes basic heeling on and off leash, and walking through a group of people. A gun is fired when the dog is off leash, and the dog will fail the trial if he is gun-shy. The dog must obey sit and down commands while heeling, as the handler continues on. On the sit command, the handler returns to the dog. On the down command, the dog will be called to the handler. Another exercise is a retrieve over a thirty-nine inch jump. The final exercise is the long down-stay, with the handler some distance away with his back to the dog. The dog remains in the down-stay position while another dog completes his exercises.

In the Protection section, a human decoy hides in a field and the dog must locate him. The dog must bark but not bite. Next, the dog, heeling off lead, must attack the decoy, who will come out of hiding to attack the dog's handler. The decoy will hit the dog with a switch, and the dog must not show fear. On command, the dog must stop his

Ch. OTCH U-UD Qazar Charfire V. Siegestor HT, TT, HIC, Am. Sch-H I, CGC, TDI, SCD, WD-X, HOF, ROM, "Select," owned by Elaine Havens. Photo by Jan Haderlie.

aggression. The decoy then runs away, acting in a belligerent manner, and the handler sends the dog after him to attack and hold.

Schutzhund II

A dog must pass Schutzhund I before attempting the requirements for the Schutzhund II degree. The three sections are the same, but the difficulty is increased.

In Tracking, the dog must find two lost articles over a strange trail, about 600 paces long and at least thirty minutes old, while on an eleven-yard lead.

The first part of the Obedience section is the same as in Schutzhund I: heeling on and off lead, proof of not being gun-shy, and a sit-stay and down-stay. Three other exercises test the dog's retrieving ability. In the first exercise, the dog retrieves a heavy wooden dumbbell over level ground. In the second, the dog retrieves a wooden dumbbell with a free jump over a forty-inch hurdle. The dog must execute a "go away," leaving his handler on command, for at least thirty paces in a fast gait in an indicated direction, and must lie down on command. This is followed by the long down-stay.

In the Protection section, the dog must first locate the decoy hiding in a field. He must bark but not bite. The handler leaves the dog to guard the "suspect" while he investigates the suspect's hiding place. The suspect then tries to escape and the dog must stop him by seizing him. When the suspect stops trying to escape, the dog must cease his aggression without a command. The suspect then tries to attack the dog with a stick, and the dog must immediately attack the suspect to prevent him from

Mex. Am. Ch. Condor V. Siegestor, UDT, PC, ET, ATD, Sch-H III, owned by Kathy Marti, flies through the air during an attack.

Mex. Am. OTCH Windstorm V. Siegestor, TD, PC, ET, ATD, Int. Sch-H III Ch., owned by Kurt Marti, is shown in Schutzhund training.

further aggression. Next, the suspect is transported, with the dog and handler about forty paces behind. After the transport, the suspect will attempt to attack the handler, and the dog must prevent the attack. In the courage exercise, the dog is sent after the suspect, who is about fifty paces away. The dog must seize the suspect and hold him firmly until called off by his handler.

Schutzhund III

This is the most advanced Schutzhund degree. The sections are the same as in Schutzhund I and II.

In Tracking, the dog must search for three lost articles on a track approximately 1,200 paces long and at least fifty minutes old. The dog may be worked off lead or on an eleven-yard lead.

In Obedience, exercises similar to those in I and II are used, with the addition of two exercises which require the dog to stand on command from a walk and from a run. The handler then returns to the dog. In other exercises, the dog must retrieve a dumbbell over flat ground, complete a free jump with a dumbbell, and climb a seventy-one-inch wall. The "go away" is similar to the Schutzhund II exercise, except that the dog must go away from his handler forty paces. The last exercise is the long down-stay with the handler fifty feet away, out of sight of his dog.

In the Protection section, the exercises are much the same as in Schutzhund II. The dog chases a suspect who strikes the dog, and the dog must subdue and hold the suspect. The dog is scored on his overall combativeness during the protection portion of this test.

Endurance Test

The test for the endurance degree (ET or AD) requires that the dog exert physical effort without exhibiting extreme fatigue. The test is held on roads and paths of as many different surfaces as possible for a distance of 12.4 miles.

There are three rest stops, at which the dogs are checked by a judge for signs of fatigue or other problems.

To be eligible for the test, a dog must be at least twelve months old and in good health and physical condition. The dog is on leash and must gait at a speed of about 6.2 miles per hour on the right side of the handler. The handler may run or ride a bicycle. The dog, on a loose lead, is allowed to pull forward but cannot lag behind for any length of time. When half of the distance has been covered, there is a ten-minute rest period.

The judge must follow the dog the entire distance and must be present at the rest period. A car is available to pick up any dog that is unable to complete the full distance.

A fifteen-minute break follows the completion of the running, and then the dog must exhibit basic obedience work, including off-lead heeling and a retrieve of a dumbbell or object over a thirty-nine-inch jump. If a dog lacks temper or toughness, shows signs of exceptional fatigue or cannot keep up a speed of six miles per hour, the examination is considered "not passed." Two hours are allowed for the completion of the endurance examination.

Ch. Esprit De Noir V. Siegestor, CDX, ET, Sch-H I. Owners, Mara Lee Jiles and Rayeann Schur.

Ch. Buena Vuk of Blue Lake, CDX, TD, ET, Sch-H I. Owners, Shane and Kathay Wagoner.

Schutzhund Trial winners, 1980: Left to right, Mex. Am. Ch. and OTCH Windstorm V. Siegestor, TD, PC, ET, ATD, Int. Sch-H III. Ch. Owner, Kurt Marti; Zorro V. Siegestor, CDX, ET, Sch-H II. Owner, Robin Smiley; Mex. Am. Ch. Condor V. Siegestor, UDT, PC, ET, ATD, Sch-H III. Owner, Kathy Marti; Ch. Esprit De Noir V. Siegestor, CDX, ET, Sch-H I. Owners, Mara Lee Jiles and Rayeann Schur; Ch. Bando V. Siegestor, CD, TD, ET, ATD. Owners, Mara Lee Jiles and Rayeann Schur.

Belgians are able to work a large flock on open grazing. Nyjella Ceres Kuymal, RD, HTRD-III-s, d, ATD-d, STD-c, HS, HGH, CGC, owned by Peggy Richter.

Herding Work and Competitions

by Peggy Richter*

THE JOB OF A HERDING DOG is simple—to manage livestock in such a way that the owner can move the stock easily and quietly where and when they want. This requires a dog that has a combination of instinct, trained skills, the ability to obey, and the ability to disobey. In the French trials, there is actually a deduction for a dog who obeys "counter to sense."[1]

BACKGROUND

The Belgian herding dogs were bred to be used as general purpose farm dogs,[2] usually working medium to large groups of sheep or cattle. Sheep in Europe were similar in breed type to the Merino, Rambollet, Cotswold, and Dorset of today; the cattle were usually dairy cattle. They were herded in unfenced areas, including the Ardennes forest.[3] These sheep were accustomed to being worked on a daily basis—taken from the fold at dawn, walked to the grazing area, and returned to the fold at night. Frequently worked stock do not react in the same way as stock left in pastures for months without being worked, as was typical in Scotland and England.[4]

Consequently, the Belgian and most sheep herding (shepherd) type dogs work in a different style than that of the modern trial Border Collie. For example, they do not generally work at great distances. They do not use "eye," staring their stock into submission, because that works best on stock unused to dogs. Instead, they manage their stock by physical closeness, preferring to be within reaching distance of their charges. This has a disadvantage when working easily frightened stock or stock unfamiliar with a dog, but is extremely useful when it comes to convincing a stubborn Suffolk that it is time to leave the pasture or a Cotswold ram that he needs to leave the ewes.

Irrespective of style is "generic" herding, the innate instinct to bunch stock together (gathering) and bring them to the handler (fetching). More than one Belgian, when first introduced to stock,

---

* *Peggy Richter was one of the first to work extensively in herding with Belgian Sheepdogs.*

has gathered the animals into very tight little knots with the handler trapped in the center—a case of excess enthusiasm! Some Belgians like to turn their stock by approaching from behind (heeling), but the majority appear to prefer going to the faces of their stock to turn them (heading). Regardless of whether his natural preference is to head or heel, the dog is later trained to take commands from a handler. The commands include: "go by" (to go clockwise); "away to me" (go counterclockwise); to move from the handler towards the stock; to "rate" (move stock at a reasonable speed); "cross-drive" (to take stock diagonally from the handler); or to "drive" (take them directly away). Perhaps the most difficult thing to teach a Belgian is to "stop." Belgians tend to be very forceful with their stock—a decided plus when you are dealing with three hundred Suffolk, but they often must be taught to tone it down for American trials using only three sheep that have had minimal exposure to a Belgian Sheepdog.[5] Many Belgians appear to have retained a significant amount of the kind of herding ability that shepherds in Belgium wanted to preserve.

HOW BELGIANS WORK

Belgians are very similar in many ways to other breeds of herding dogs that are called "loose-eyed and upright." Many people are familiar with a Border Collie creeping up on stock, belly almost to the ground, intensely staring at the animals he is working. Belgians are not like this. Their approach is made standing up, openly, without an intense stare. In comparison, the Border Collie approaches like a fox, the Belgian like a wolf. It is not that Belgians never stare, but that they do not use the stare to fixate on or to intimidate the stock. Their size, appearance and confident manner gives them all the authority they need. They generally do not work far away from their stock. On both sheep and cattle, Belgians tend to work "close," sometimes close enough to touch the

Belgians work close. Here Kuymal is turning the flock.

stock. By inclination, Belgians will only stay as far away from the stock as they must in order to work the stock properly.

Many Belgians seem to have more of a "management" view of the stock than a predatory one. Rather than seeing the stock as "lunch" that they are bringing to the handler, they often seem to view the stock as odd, subordinate pack members. Often, when stock do not behave the way the dog expects them to, the same disciplinary behavior is exhibited as if the stock were misbehaving subordinate dogs. Belgians are very "order-oriented." Their inclination is to have the stock grouped in a nice orderly pack or to have the stock moving in a nice orderly group. Individual animals that are not "part of the program" are quickly spotted and disciplined. Like many breeds used to move stock in the open, Belgians tend to be very insistent that *all* of the animals be together—which can make separating out stock or leaving animals behind difficult. Of course, Belgian Sheepdogs are individuals, so not all will perform herding duties in exactly the same way

The breed Standard in both the original Belgian standard and in the AKC versions mentions that Belgians tend to move in a circle rather than a straight line. There is a reason for this. Belgians will circle the flock or herd, bunching them together and keeping them grouped. When traveling on a path, down a road, or through a course, there is a strong tendency for Belgian Sheepdogs to "push" from behind, then come to the side to make sure that none of the animals are slipping out on the sides. They will then tend to check the front to ensure no stock are stampeding away, check the other side to make sure none are escaping there, and finally return to the rear for another "push."

A well-trained Belgian can move stock on the open road without panic or flight.

In medium to large flocks and medium-sized herds this method works very well indeed when using a single dog, as it is the most efficient means of covering all sides of the group to ensure the stock stay together and are moving in the correct direction. This was considered such an important characteristic that it became the only herding-specific behavior ever written in a breed standard.

Belgians also tend to have a lot of "presence" on stock. This is because the general use was to employ one dog on flocks of up to 200 sheep and medium-sized herds of five to twenty cattle. The sheep in Belgium were often used for dairy, and almost all flocks were worked on a daily basis, being moved from pen to grazing field each day rather than turned "out" onto a pasture. Cattle were also worked in this manner. Because Belgium had no wild or feral cattle, the Belgian herding dogs were not bred to work extremely difficult cattle. Prior to the time breed standards were first written, the distinguishing factors between "cattle herder" (bouvier) and "sheep herder" (berger) were not as clear cut, so Belgian Sheepdogs do well on both sheep and cooperative cattle.

Stock should not run. Kuymal is learning to circle the goats and to stay an appropriate distance from them. Photo © Kent and Donna Dannen.

This dog is quietly moving three Cotswold lambs. Chieho's X-XU Rocket, HTD-III-d, Std-d,s, HGH, CGC, owned by Peggy Richter.

Despite the popularity and publicity of the Border Collie, the Belgians have more than held their own in herding in the United States. In the AKC and American Herding Breed Association programs, they have had a higher percentage of dogs earning titles and earning the highest titles in relationship to number of dogs registered than any other breed (AKC statistics, AHBA records 1990-2000).

HOW TO GET STARTED IN HERDING

If you are interested in herding with your Belgian, the first task is to decide what work the dog is to perform. It is unfair to a dog of any type to ask it to work in one style most of the time and compete in another. If you want to compete in Border Collie trials, you should try to avoid spending all your

Nyjella Ceres Kuymal, RD, HTRD-III-s,d, ATD-d, STD-c, HS, HGH, CGC, owned by Peggy Richter, is moving cattle through a panel at an ASCA (Australian Shepherd Club of America) trial.

time training in arenas. Belgians used to working large flocks of heavy Suffolk sheep may find it difficult to translate their herding ability into working three head of frightened Barbadoe at an AKC test.

Once you have determined what you want, your next task is to find a trainer who has dogs that work in that same way. You will need to take lessons under an experienced herding trainer. If he or she has worked with the Belgian breeds, so much the better. Most trainers keep their own stock or are associated with a club that maintains livestock for herding purposes. By joining the club or class you will probably have access to livestock and facilities in which to practice between lessons. You do not necessarily need to live on a farm and keep your own livestock in order to enjoy herding and to compete in tests and trials. Herding does, however, require a lot of dedication and training time, but it is extremely fulfilling to watch your Belgian joyfully perform the task he was bred to do.

Many Belgian Sheepdog owners are hobbyists who compete in herding tests or trials on a novice level for fun. Some breeders hope to preserve herding instinct in their bloodlines by testing or trialing their breeding stock. Belgians also continue to serve as working stock dogs. (Contrary to popular myth, there are probably more dogs working stock now than there were in the 1800s.) There are plenty of places for a general purpose farm dog with the ability to work sheep or cattle all day and join the family on the couch in the evening. The Belgian Sheepdog is an excellent choice for people with small farms and ranches who are desirous of a quality stockdog. Since herding is an hereditary trait, the best way to get a good herding dog is to look for a pup out of good herding parents with titles in the type of work in which you want to compete.

A Belgian Sheepdog competing in a herding trial. Right: driving through a gate. Below: bringing the sheep down the fence. Photos © Judith Strom.

HERDING PROGRAMS

Numerous herding programs are available to Belgian Sheepdogs. Each of the organizations has slightly different rules and regulations. Since regulations are subject to change, it is always advisable to check with the organizations to make sure you are training under current rules.

- *The American Herding Breed Association* (AHBA) sponsors tests that are open to all dogs of herding ancestry and their trials are open to all dogs that can perform the work.
- *The American Kennel Club* (AKC) sponsors tests and trials open to all registered AKC-recognized herding breeds.
- *The Australian Shepherd Club of America* (ASCA) trials are open to all registered herding breeds.
- *Herdenhunde of North America* (HGH) is affiliated with United Schutzhund Clubs of America and holds trials that are open to any dog that can perform the work.
- A number of different *Border Collie clubs* hold trials open to any breed that

COMPARISON OF HERDING TITLES

American Kennel Club
- HT — Herding Tested
- PT — Pre-Trial Tested
- HS — Herding Started
- HI — Herding Intermediate
- HE — Herding Excellent
- HCH — Herding Champion

American Herding Breed Association
- HCT — Herding Capability Tested
- JHD — Junior Herding (similar to AKC Pre-Trial)
- HTD-I — Herding Trial Dog Level 1
- HTD-II — Herding Trial Dog Level 2 (increases in difficulty)
- HTD-III — Herding Trial Dog Level 3
- HRD — Herding Ranch Dog (also in three levels)
- HTCh — Herding Trial Champion

AHBA titles are awarded according to type of stock (ducks, sheep, and cattle) designated by the letter d, s, or c following the title.

Australian Shepherd Club of America
- STD — Started Trial Dog
- OTD — Open Trial Dog
- ATD — Advanced Trial Dog
- WTCh — Working Trial Champion

ASCA uses the designation -s after the title to indicate sheep, -d to indicate ducks, and -c to indicate that the title was achieved by working cattle.

ENDNOTES:

[1] *French herding trial rules, translated by Linda Rorem, printed September 1995, AHBA.*

[2] *Von Stephanitz,* The German Shepherd in Word and Picture, *1927, various photographs of early Belgians, record of 1893 herding trial in Belgium (translated by Linda Rorem),* The Berger Belge Anthology, *verbal correspondence with various representatives of the Belgian clubs in Europe.*

[3] *Ibid.*

[4] *Gillflan* SHEEP, *1927; discussions with Ernest Hartnagle, Linda Rorem, et al.* The Golden Hoof, The Saga of Fort Tejon, America's Sheep Trails, SHEEP, *experiments conducted at Kuymal Ranch.*

[5] *Vergil Holland.*

An adult Belgian Sheepdog with a young puppy. Photo © Kent and Donna Dannen.

Chapter Eleven

Breeding and Whelping

BREEDING PUREBRED DOGS IS not to be entered into lightly. Too many inferior-quality dogs are bred in America today, and many good individuals end up in shelters waiting for a new home. This is especially true of working and herding breed dogs that sometimes have difficulty fitting into our sedentary, urban society. Raising dogs is hard work and very time-consuming, and you are not likely to make a profit—especially if you hold the best interest of the breed at heart. In a very few short weeks, the body, nervous system, and intelligence of the puppies all develop at the same time. They become little adults, but they lack experience and need socialization and training to fulfill their potential. They will learn one way or another, and if unguided their behavior may be less than desirable. Remember, Belgians are an active, intelligent breed that needs something to do. This trait begins to surface at a very early age. Bad habits are hard to correct once established, and your wonderful puppies, through no fault of their own, can end up in a pound. We know some dogs that go to shelters are products of poor breeding and inherited problems, but irresponsible people also can ruin the best dog that ever lived. If you aren't willing to make the commitment of time, money, and energy required, you should consider some other way to enjoy your dogs instead of breeding them.

Let's assume you are serious about preserving and improving the characteristics of the breed. Before you attempt to breed a litter of Belgians, you should study the breed history and pedigrees, observe the different bloodlines for yourself, and talk with a host of long-time breeders to learn all you can about type, temperament, faults, and virtues in the various lines.

Then, you should select the best female you can possibly afford—one that has been checked for all hereditary problems and found to be clear. A potential brood bitch, regardless of breed, should have good bone, ample breadth and depth of ribbing, and adequate room in the pelvic region. Your bitch should be a good representative of the breed Standard. If she has any disqualifying faults, she should not be bred at all. You must observe her carefully so that you know

Using colored ribbons can help identify the puppies. Be sure to use "stretchy" material and check often so that the ribbons are not too tight as puppies grow. Breeder, Pat Snow.

her strong points, as well as what she is lacking, in order to find a stud dog that will improve the qualities she lacks and not introduce new faults.

It takes time and experience to learn all of this. Go to shows and visit with breeders (after they have finished showing) to learn more about pedigrees and breed quality. The results of a mating are not always what you anticipate. The science of genetics is complex and often unpredictable. Never rush to breed to a "popular" dog until you investigate the quality of his offspring and can anticipate the results of such a union.

THE BROOD BITCH

The breeding life of a bitch begins when she comes into season the first time at the age of eight to ten months. Thereafter, she will come in season at roughly six-month intervals. Her maximum fertility builds up from puberty to full maturity and then declines until a state of total sterility is reached in old age. Just when this occurs is difficult to determine, for the fact that an older bitch shows signs of being in season does not necessarily mean she is still capable of reproducing.

Although a Belgian Sheepdog bitch may come in season before a year old, I prefer not to breed her until she is at least two years old. Furthermore, even though it is possible for a bitch to conceive twice a year, she should not be bred more than once a year. A bitch that is bred too often will age prematurely and her puppies are likely to lack vigor.

The length of the heat season varies from eighteen to twenty-one days. The first indication is a pronounced swelling of the vulva with coincidental bleeding (called "showing color") for about the first seven to nine days. The discharge gradually turns to a cream color, and it is during this phase (estrus), from about the tenth to fifteenth day, that the bitch ovulates and is receptive to the male. The ripe, unfertilized ova survive for about seventy-two hours. If fertilization doesn't occur, the ova die and are discharged. If fertilization does take place, each ovum attaches itself to the wall of the uterus, a membrane forms to seal it off, and a fetus develops.

Following the estrus phase, the bitch is still in season until about the twenty-first day and will continue to be attractive to males, although she will usually fight them off as she did the first few days. Nevertheless, to avoid accidental mating, the bitch must be confined for the entire period. Virtual imprisonment is necessary, for male dogs display uncanny abilities in their efforts to reach a bitch in season.

The odor that attracts the males is present in the bitch's urine, so it is advisable to take her a good distance from the house before permitting her to relieve herself. To eliminate problems completely, your veterinarian can prescribe a preparation that will disguise the odor but will not interfere with breeding when the time is right. Many fanciers use such preparations when exhibiting a bitch and find that nearby males show no interest whatsoever. But it is not advisable to permit a bitch to run loose when she has been given a product of this type, for during estrus she will seek the company of male dogs and an accidental mating still can occur.

Two or three months before a bitch is to be mated, her physical condition should be considered carefully. If she is too thin, provide a rich, balanced diet plus enough regular exercise to develop strong, supple muscles. Daily exercise on leash is as necessary for the too-thin bitch as for the too-fat one, although the latter will need more exercise and at a brisker pace, as well as a reduction of food, to bring her to optimum condition. A prospective brood bitch must be current on all the usual vaccinations. A month before her season is due, a veterinarian should examine a stool specimen for worms. If there is evidence of infestation, the bitch should be treated with the appropriate wormer.

The first time your bitch is bred, it is preferable to use a stud that has already proven his siring ability. The fact that a neighbor's dog is readily available should not influence your choice. In order to produce the best puppies, you must select the stud most suitable from a genetic standpoint. Begin your search for the right stud well in advance of your

THE FEMALE REPRODUCTIVE SYSTEM

The female reproductive system consists of the ovaries, uterine tubes, uterus, vagina, and vulva, as illustrated.

The ovaries are responsible for egg production, and are also the source of certain hormones. The ovaries of the newborn bitch contain her lifetime supply of eggs—hundreds of thousands.

After ovulation the eggs pass through the tubes into the uterus. Each tube is also about the size of a two-inch section of spaghetti. Unlike most mammals, in the dog fertilization takes place in the uterine tubes, and the fertilized eggs remain there for about six days before moving to the uterine horn.

The uterus is "Y" shaped, and during pregnancy the developing fetuses are distributed between the two horns. The uterus is divided into three areas: the horns, the body, and the cervix. The horns lead to the body of the uterus, which is the passageway to the vagina. The cervix, lying at the base of the uterus, is the doorway. On one side of it lies the uterus, the ideal environment for the incubation of the fertilized eggs. On the other side lies the vagina, the opening to the outside.

The vulva is the external genitalia of the female. The lips of the vulva swell and become puffy during estrus.

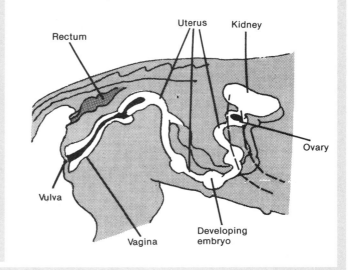

bitch's next heat cycle. A good place to look is at the local shows, or by contacting members of a local breed club if there is one. You can also look at magazine ads and ask the breeder who sold you your bitch for recommendations.

When you find the right male, discuss the stud fee, how early in the cycle they would like you to bring your bitch, what tests might be required prior to breeding, and whether they will provide a repeat service if the bitch does not get pregnant. Usually the first service will be successful. However, if it isn't, in most cases an additional service is given free, provided the stud dog is still in the possession of the same owner. If the bitch misses, it may be because her cycle varies widely from normal. Your veterinarian can determine exactly when the bitch is entering the estrus phase and thus is likely to conceive by doing a microscopic examination of swabs taken during the heat cycle.

The owner of the stud should give you a stud service certificate showing the date of the mating, and provide a four-generation pedigree for the sire. The litter registration application is completed only after the puppies are whelped, but it, too, must be signed by the owner of the stud as well as the owner of the bitch. Registration forms may be secured by writing the American Kennel Club or can be downloaded from their online website.

THE STUD DOG

Owning a stud dog is not a good choice for a beginning breeder. If you own a bitch, you can try different studs with her, shipping her anywhere in the country if necessary. A male dog can produce many more offspring than a bitch, and an inferior dog, or one who carries recessive genes for an undesirable trait, can adversely affect the breed for many generations. Wait until you have plenty of experience before taking the responsibility for owning a stud dog.

A male can be used at stud from the time he reaches physical maturity well into old age. In the Belgian this is usually about twelve months of age through about twelve years. If the sire is older than twelve years, the AKC will require proof that he was the actual sire of the litter. You should be aware that the AKC requires DNA certification for males that sire seven or more litters in a lifetime, or more than three litters in a calendar year. This is used for genetic identity and parentage verification.

PREGNANCY

The gestation period for a bitch is nine weeks (63 days), but it can vary from sixty-one to sixty-five days without cause for concern. If it goes beyond sixty-five days from the date of mating, a veterinarian should be consulted. In normal pregnancy, visible enlargement of the abdomen usually occurs by the end of the fifth week. A veterinarian may be able to distinguish developing puppies as early as three weeks after mating by palpating the abdomen, but it is unwise for a novice to poke and prod trying to detect the presence of unborn puppies. If you really need to know, have your veterinarian examine your bitch with ultrasound, which can detect puppies early after breeding.

During the first four or five weeks of her pregnancy, the bitch should be permitted her normal amount of activity. As she becomes heavier, she should be walked on leash, and strenuous running and jumping should be avoided. Her diet should be well balanced, and if she

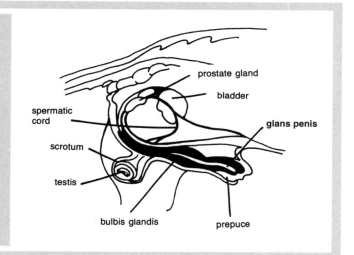

THE MALE REPRODUCTIVE SYSTEM

The male reproductive system of the dog is unique in that the bulbis glandis enlarges after intromission. The swelling of this gland locks the dog and bitch together until ejaculation has taken place. This "tie" may last anywhere from five to thirty minutes or more.

become constipated, small amounts of mineral oil may be added to her food.

About two weeks before the puppies are due, move the mother-to-be to a whelping box. The bitch should use it as her bed so she will be accustomed to it by the time puppies arrive. Preferably, the box should be square, with each side long enough so that the bitch can stretch out full length with several inches to spare at either end. The bottom should be padded with an old cotton rug or other material that is easily laundered. Tack the edges of the padding to the floor of the box so the puppies will not get caught in it and smother. Once it is obvious that labor is about to begin, the padding should be covered with several layers of spread-out newspapers. As the paper becomes soiled, the top layer can be pulled off, leaving the area clean.

WHELPING

Forty-eight to seventy-two hours before the bitch goes into labor you will probably notice a definite change in the shape of the abdomen. Instead of looking barrel-shaped, the abdomen will sag pendulously. Breasts usually redden and become enlarged, and milk may be present a day or two before the puppies are whelped. As the time becomes imminent, the bitch will scratch and root at her bedding in an effort to make a nest, and will probably refuse food and ask to be let out frequently. A drop in temperature of two or three degrees approximately twelve hours before labor begins is one of the surest signs that labor is approaching.

The bitch's abdomen and flanks will contract sharply when labor starts, and for a few minutes she will attempt to expel a puppy, then rest and try again. Someone should stay with the bitch the entire time whelping is taking place, and should call a veterinarian if she appears to be having unusual difficulties.

Puppies are usually born head first, although some arrive feet first with no difficulty. Each puppy is enclosed in a separate membranous sac that the bitch will remove with her teeth. She will sever the umbilical cord, which will be attached to the soft, spongy afterbirth that is expelled right after the puppy emerges. Usually the bitch eats the afterbirth, so it is necessary to watch and make sure one is expelled for each

Date bred	Date due to whelp	Date bred	Date due to whelp	Date bred	Date due to whelp	Date bred	Date due to whelp	Date bred	Date due to whelp	Date bred	Date due to whelp	Date bred	Date due to whelp	Date bred	Date due to whelp	Date bred	Date due to whelp	Date bred	Date due to whelp	Date bred	Date due to whelp	Date bred	Date due to whelp
January	March	February	April	March	May	April	June	May	July	June	August	July	September	August	October	September	November	October	December	November	January	December	February
1	5	1	5	1	3	1	3	1	3	1	3	1	2	1	3	1	3	1	3	1	3	1	2
2	6	2	6	2	4	2	4	2	4	2	4	2	3	2	4	2	4	2	4	2	4	2	3
3	7	3	7	3	5	3	5	3	5	3	5	3	4	3	5	3	5	3	5	3	5	3	4
4	8	4	8	4	6	4	6	4	6	4	6	4	5	4	6	4	6	4	6	4	6	4	5
5	9	5	9	5	7	5	7	5	7	5	7	5	6	5	7	5	7	5	7	5	7	5	6
6	10	6	10	6	8	6	8	6	8	6	8	6	7	6	8	6	8	6	8	6	8	6	7
7	11	7	11	7	9	7	9	7	9	7	9	7	8	7	9	7	9	7	9	7	9	7	8
8	12	8	12	8	10	8	10	8	10	8	10	8	9	8	10	8	10	8	10	8	10	8	9
9	13	9	13	9	11	9	11	9	11	9	11	9	10	9	11	9	11	9	11	9	11	9	10
10	14	10	14	10	12	10	12	10	12	10	12	10	11	10	12	10	12	10	12	10	12	10	11
11	15	11	15	11	13	11	13	11	13	11	13	11	12	11	13	11	13	11	13	11	13	11	12
12	16	12	16	12	14	12	14	12	14	12	14	12	13	12	14	12	14	12	14	12	14	12	13
13	17	13	17	13	15	13	15	13	15	13	15	13	14	13	15	13	15	13	15	13	15	13	14
14	18	14	18	14	16	14	16	14	16	14	16	14	15	14	16	14	16	14	16	14	16	14	15
15	19	15	19	15	17	15	17	15	17	15	17	15	16	15	17	15	17	15	17	15	17	15	16
16	20	16	20	16	18	16	18	16	18	16	18	16	17	16	18	16	18	16	18	16	18	16	17
17	21	17	21	17	19	17	19	17	19	17	19	17	18	17	19	17	19	17	19	17	19	17	18
18	22	18	22	18	20	18	20	18	20	18	20	18	19	18	20	18	20	18	20	18	20	18	19
19	23	19	23	19	21	19	21	19	21	19	21	19	20	19	21	19	21	19	21	19	21	19	20
20	24	20	24	20	22	20	22	20	22	20	22	20	21	20	22	20	22	20	22	20	22	20	21
21	25	21	25	21	23	21	23	21	23	21	23	21	22	21	23	21	23	21	23	21	23	21	22
22	26	22	26	22	24	22	24	22	24	22	24	22	23	22	24	22	24	22	24	22	24	22	23
23	27	23	27	23	25	23	25	23	25	23	25	23	24	23	25	23	25	23	25	23	25	23	24
24	28	24	28	24	26	24	26	24	26	24	26	24	25	24	26	24	26	24	26	24	26	24	25
25	29	25	29	25	27	25	27	25	27	25	27	25	26	25	27	25	27	25	27	25	27	25	26
26	30	26	30	26	28	26	28	26	28	26	28	26	27	26	28	26	28	26	28	26	28	26	27
27	31	27	May 1	27	29	27	29	27	29	27	29	27	28	27	29	27	29	27	29	27	29	27	28
28	Apr. 1	28	2	28	30	28	30	28	30	28	30	28	29	28	30	28	30	28	30	28	30	28	Mar. 1
29	2			29	31	29	July 1	29	31	29	31	29	30	29	31	29	Dec. 1	29	31	29	31	29	2
30	3			30	June 1	30	2	30	Aug. 1	30	Sep. 1	30	Oct. 1	30	Nov. 1	30	2	30	Jan. 1	30	Feb. 1	30	3
31	4			31	2			31	2			31	2	31	2			31	2			31	4

Whelping Chart.

puppy whelped. If an afterbirth is retained, the bitch can develop peritonitis and die. If you are not sure every afterbirth was expelled during whelping, take your bitch to the veterinarian as soon as possible.

The dam will lick and nuzzle each newborn puppy until it is warm and dry and ready to nurse. If puppies arrive so close together that she can't take care of them, you can help her by rubbing the puppies dry with a soft cloth. If several have been whelped but the bitch continues to be in labor, all but one should be removed and placed in a small box lined with clean towels and warmed to about 85° F. The bitch will be calmer if one puppy is left with her at all times.

Whelping sometimes continues as long as twenty-four hours for a very large litter, but a litter of two or three puppies may be whelped in an hour. Seven or eight Belgian Sheepdog puppies could be considered an average litter, although actual litter size might range from two to thirteen. When the bitch settles down, curls around the puppies and nuzzles them close to her and sleeps, it usually indicates that all puppies have been whelped.

The bitch should be taken away for a few minutes while you clean the box and arrange clean padding. If her coat is soiled, sponge it clean before she returns to the puppies. Once she is back in the box, offer her a bowl of warm beef broth and a pan of cool water, placing both where she will not have to get up in order to reach them. As soon as she indicates interest in food, give her a generous bowl of chopped meat to which cod-liver oil and dicalcium phosphate have been added.

If inadequate amounts of calcium are provided during the period the puppies are nursing, eclampsia may develop. Symptoms are violent trembling, rapid

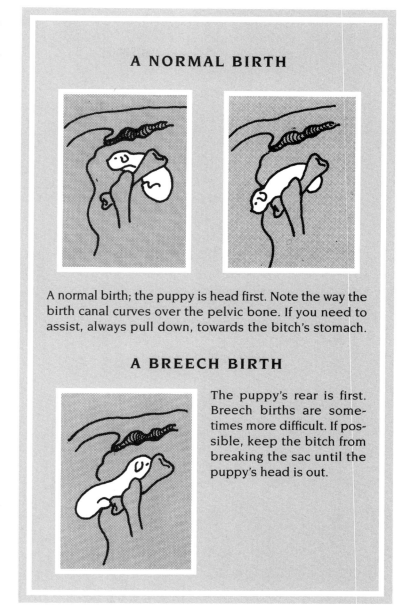

A NORMAL BIRTH

A normal birth; the puppy is head first. Note the way the birth canal curves over the pelvic bone. If you need to assist, always pull down, towards the bitch's stomach.

A BREECH BIRTH

The puppy's rear is first. Breech births are sometimes more difficult. If possible, keep the bitch from breaking the sac until the puppy's head is out.

rise in temperature, and rigidity of muscles. Veterinary assistance must be secured immediately, for death can result in a very short time. Treatment consists of massive doses of calcium gluconate administered intravenously, after which symptoms subside in a miraculously short time.

For weak or very small puppies, supplemental feeding is often recommended. Any one of three different methods may be used: tube-feeding (with a catheter attached to a syringe), using an eyedropper (this method requires great care in order to avoid getting formula in the lungs), or using a tiny bottle (the "pet nurser" available at most pet supply stores). Commercially prepared puppy formulas such as Esbilac are most convenient and are readily obtainable from a veterinarian, who can also tell you which method of administering the formula is most practical in your particular case. It is important to remember that equipment must be kept scrupulously clean. It can be sterilized by boiling, or it may be soaked in a Clorox solution, then washed carefully and dried between feedings.

CARE OF THE LITTER

All puppies are born blind. Their eyes open when they are ten to fourteen days old. At first the eyes have a bluish cast and appear weak. The puppies must be protected from strong light until at least ten days after their eyes open.

To ensure proper emotional development, young dogs should be shielded from loud noises and rough handling. Being lifted by the front legs is painful and may result in permanent injury to the shoulders. So when lifting a puppy, always place one hand under his chest with the forefinger between the front legs, and place the other hand under his bottom.

Flannelized rubber sheeting is an ideal surface for the bottom of the bed for the new puppies. It is inexpensive and washable, and will provide a surface that will give the puppies traction so that they will not slip either while nursing or when learning to walk.

Sometimes the puppies' nails are so long and sharp that they scratch the bitch's breasts. Since the nails are soft, they can be trimmed with ordinary nail clippers for the first few weeks.

A whelping box with a contented mama and full of sleeping puppies is a pretty picture. The whelping is over and everyone is relaxed and happy. The room is warm, about 85° F, which is about right for the first week of the puppies' life. They nurse, sleep, and cuddle up with their littermates and their mother. The mother constantly massages the puppies by licking them with her tongue, not only to keep them clean, but to cause them to eliminate, for puppies at birth and many days afterwards are not able to eliminate on their own. The first twenty-one days are a critical period for survival for the puppies.

After the first three weeks, things begin to change. The puppies become aware of their surroundings. They can see, smell, hear, and move around. This is an interesting time to watch them. Their muscles are not very coordinated

Four-week-old puppy bred by Laura Patton.

Six-week-old puppy, Ch. Sherborne Fresh Heir, breeder Jill Sherer.

yet and their play and fights with each other are comical to watch. They need this time in their life to form attachment to their mother and littermates. They also need a combination of socializing with other dogs and human beings. Lacking this, they may form an attachment to one or the other, which can influence them later in life.

Keep their toenails checked, and snip or blunt the sharp points on the end with a file for the comfort of the nursing mother.

WEANING

At about four weeks of age, the puppies can be started on formula. You can feed one of the commercially prepared formulas according to the directions on the container, or prepare a homemade version in accordance with instructions from a veterinarian. Warm the formula to lukewarm and pour it into a shallow pan placed on the floor of the box. You may have to dip the puppies' mouths into the mixture a few times, after which they will usually start to lap the formula. All puppies should eat from the same pan, but be sure the small ones get their share. If they are pushed aside, feed them separately. Increase the amount fed each day over a period of two weeks. At six weeks the puppies can be weaned completely. Continue to permit the puppies to nurse, but gradually increase the amount of formula and feeding times until the puppies are getting four meals a day. Then gradually begin to blend or crush dry puppy food and mix it with the formula.

By the time you start feeding the puppies, they should be accustomed to being handled by the breeder and familiar with the human smell. It is now time

Littermates need to socialize with each other and to have plenty of room to play. Breeder, Pat Snow.

Time out! Puppies play hard, but need lots of rest. Breeder, Pat Snow.

brush his belly while talking to him in a soothing tone. The tone of your voice is important while handling a puppy. A soft, reassuring voice gives the puppy a calming sensation and a secure feeling of being loved.

Make the session short the first time. This extra attention gives each puppy the confidence he needs as an individual. As he becomes familiar with being handled and brushed, you can do more grooming and gradually raise the height of the grooming surface until he learns to stand on a grooming table.

By the time the puppies are five weeks old, the dam should be allowed with them only at night. At about six weeks old, they should be weaned completely. Three meals a day are usually sufficient from this time until the puppies are six months old, when feedings can be reduced to two a day. About the time the dog reaches one year of age, you can reduce the feeding to once a day if you desire.

The puppies will need a temporary distemper and parvovirus vaccination at six weeks, followed by a series of two or three more inoculations four weeks apart until they are old enough for their permanent shots. Stool specimens should be checked for worms when the puppies are six weeks old because, almost without exception, puppies become infested. Specimens should be checked again at eight weeks, and as often thereafter as your veterinarian recommends.

Do not bathe young puppies unless they get into some offensive material that you can't easily remove. You can lightly spray them with your spray bottle using warm water or a "waterless" shampoo and then dry them with a soft towel. Never use an adult shampoo or flea spray on young puppies as their skin is very tender and can't stand harsh chemicals of any kind. Human baby

to take them out of the whelping box individually and spend some time playing with each one. The best way to begin is on the floor away from the whelping box. A puppy is afraid of height at first, so the floor is safe footing and provides a comfortable level for the two of you. Use a soft brush and playfully brush the puppy. Roll him over on his back and

shampoo or gentle organic shampoos are usually safe, although you may want to check with your veterinarian.

If you have investigated and eliminated potential hereditary problems, then proper nutrition and other environmental factors, such as good footing in the whelping box (as well as later on) should be all that is needed to avoid developmental problems. Puppies raised on a slick surface may be more prone to hip dysplasia than those raised under better conditions. Proper diet is very important to the development of a strong-bodied pup. Since a puppy's bones are soft, in my opinion you should avoid throwing something in the air and having the puppy jump for it. If you notice a puppy behaving in an unusual manner, discuss the symptoms with your veterinarian and follow his advice.

SOMETHING TO THINK ABOUT

When you think about how fast a puppy develops and how much you can do to help them learn and adjust at crucial times which will affect them for the rest of their lives, you will realize that having a litter of puppies is a big responsibility. Breeders that take the time to bond with their puppies and give them special attention will give them a better chance to adjust to a new home. I hope that, if you choose to become a breeder, you will be *dedicated* enough to support and promote this breed which is capable of giving so much to mankind.

Marge Turnquist with Desi and sister Dazzle, bred by Kaye Hall.

Ch. Sherborne Heir Power, CD, at six weeks of age. Bred by Jill Sherer.

Young puppies need to explore a wide variety of environments. Photo courtesy of Pat Snow.

When a puppy is eight to ten weeks old his ears start to stand up. However, they may twist and flop in all directions before finally becoming erect.

How exciting it is to see your puppy win his first ribbon! Sandevel's Mirror Image bred by Sandra King. Photo © Perry Phillips.

Chapter Twelve

Pillars in the Breed

FOLLOWING ARE BRIEF SKETCHES of the some of the charter members of the BSCA and their dogs, vital participants in the reorganization of the Belgian Sheepdog Club of America, Inc.

W. B. Vestal was a member of the first Belgian Sheepdog Club of America and a charter member of the reorganized BSCA in 1947. He and his wife bred many fine Belgians and were active in showing their dogs in both conformation shows and obedience classes. Mrs. Vestal was probably best known for training and showing Ch. Hadji de Flanders, UDT, the first Belgian to be granted the two highest titles at that time, Utility Dog and Utility Dog Tracking. Hadji was trained not only for shows but also for the most important job—usefulness in everyday living. Hadji won his tracking title in his ninth year and his championship the next year—quite a feat for a dog at that age. He was trained for Red Cross rescue work, participated in exhibitions to recruit dogs for defense, and entertained wounded G.I.s in hospitals. Hadji, assisted by Mrs. Vestal, collected subscription pledges for Guide Dogs for the Blind. They were a wonderful combination of a lady and her dog giving selflessly to others.

Rush and Shirley Brown got their first Belgian, Ch. Fleur Ebon de Beaute Noir, CD, from Art and Bea Brindel of Muncie, Indiana. The Browns were charter members of the present BSCA. They have maintained a kennel of the highest quality Belgian Sheepdogs for many years. They both were active club members, showing in both conformation and obedience, and their record of achievements in all fields of endeavor is second to none. Their devotion to the breed and to high standards made their role in the advancement of the breed a very important one.

Most people in the fancy are familiar with Ch. Fume Noir, CD, "Smokey," as he was called, who was one of the Brown's foundation dogs and who played an important part in establishing their line.

In 1948, **Rush Brown, Arthur Brindel, and E. W. Hauser** were appointed by the Club to research the history of the breed for a booklet for club members. E. W. Hauser took on the job of researching literature and reference material for facts about the breed. Rush Brown and Arthur. Brindel worked back through former breeders and followed the chain of imports back to Belgium and France. This exhaustive search for facts took the three people eighteen months. They compiled the material, and the booklet was printed. Very few people realize how much effort these dedicated people expended for the club.

Rudy Robinson probably put more resources into importing good strains of Belgian Sheepdogs from Europe than any other breeder of his time. He promoted the breed through advertising in dog magazines, pamphlets on the breed, and a newsletter for his customers. Some of his well-known dogs include: Sheba III de Beaute Noir, UD, who appeared in many of his ads; Vicky and Vivette du Mont Sara; Billy von Lercenberg; and Champions Yedo, Zuzu de L'Infernal, Zita de L'Infernal, Zulvo, Arta du Chemin des Dames, and Gama des Ardennes du Coitron. He also imported an entire litter from the Pirata Nero Kennels in Italy, owned by Angelo Colombo. This litter of five dogs and two bitches was sired by Zordoff, a dog proclaimed "Champion of Italy."

Zordoff was a half-brother of Ch. Zulvo, CD, Rudy's well-known imported dog and the producer of many champions. Rudy wanted to buy Zordoff but the dog was not for sale for any amount of money. Rudy Robinson and Orrin Stine began corresponding with Mr. Colombo in an attempt to secure a couple of fine specimens sired by Zordoff. Mr. Colombo was so conscientious in his desire to supply the right specimens that he wrote Robinson and Stine a letter which said, "In order to be sure that you get the best specimens, I am going to ship you the entire litter." This was a bit more than they had bargained for, but the deal was made and the twelve-week-old litter was shipped. In that litter were two Belgians with which most people are familiar: Ch. Liza del Pirata Nero, CD (who became the Queen Mother of the Geier Tal Kennels in Oklahoma, owned by the Turnquists), and Ch. Tazir III del Pirata Nero, owned by Ted and Freda Rowland of Roll In Kennels.

Mr. Colombo bought up the best specimens of the now disbanded Mont Sara Kennels of Belgium, with the aim of preserving the fast-disappearing small ear. The small, correct ears were quite evident in his dogs and in the litter that he sent Rudy Robinson.

Mr. Colombo was presented with a full-size bronze replica of a Belgian Sheepdog for his integrity in breeding and his dedication to the breed.

With the acquisition by Rudy Robinson of the Pirata Nero line, Groenendaels from Switzerland, Belgium, Italy, and France were placed under one kennel roof. Each specimen represented Europe's best bloodlines, with characteristics that American breeders wanted to introduce into their strains. One interesting observation made to Rudy Robinson by a foreign breeder who had observed American Belgians was, "Push down those ears until the chest drops another inch."

Ted and Freda Rowland of Roll In Kennels purchased their first Belgian, Ch. Vicki de Beaute Noir, from Art and Bea Brindel in 1945. This beginning led to over thirty years of breeding and training Belgian Sheepdogs. Their many champions and fine breeding stock were well known by the Belgian fancy. They were charter members of the present parent club and worked in all club activities to help organize the club and promote the breed. In 1955, they acquired Ch. Tazir III del Pirata Nero from Rudy Robinson. "Ricky," as he was called, passed on squareness, small ears, and beautiful straight coats to his progeny, traits which were needed at that time. He was a great asset to Roll In Kennels. In 1957, the Rowlands formed a partnership with **Sam and Freda Chandler,** and the kennel name became Roll In & C. The merger of the two kennels produced many fine Belgians which placed in Groups and were Best of Breed at the National Specialty shows.

Freda Rowland was a familiar sight in the show ring. She was a remarkable person. She was familiar with all the Belgians at that time and could remember the name of the breeder of any Belgian and recite the dog's pedigree from memory. She was called the "walking encyclopedia of the breed." She never was too busy to answer letters and give advice and encouragement to beginners. The latchstring was always out at the Rowlands'. Freda was an excellent cook and nothing pleased her more than having old friends around the table to dine and to discuss dogs.

Freda Rowland died in 1970 at a National Specialty, and since 1971 a Freda Rowland Memorial Trophy, in the form of a large silver bowl, has been given by the BSCA in her memory. Each year this bowl graces the trophy table at the National Specialty, and a smaller replica is given the BOB winner. The name of the winning dog is engraved on the memorial trophy.

Roll In Kennels are gone now, but Roll In and Roll In & C dogs' names still appear on pedigrees all over the country.

Arthur and Beatrice Brindel became interested in Belgian Sheepdogs in 1942. Their stock came from a pair of Belgians from the kennels of Mrs. Cecil Lutz. The first Belgian Sheepdog to become an American champion after World War II was a bitch bred by the Brindels, Ch. Dianne de Beaute Noir, CDX. Many more champions came from the Black Beauty Kennels. Ch. Dianne de Beaute Noir, CDX, is credited with being the first bitch to acquire the CDX title.

Beatrice Brindel became Secretary/Treasurer of the reorganized BSCA in 1947 and remained in that position for several years. The Brindels were very active exhibitors and served in many capacities in the reorganized club. Many of the charter members give them credit for being an important force in holding the club together when it was trying to gain recognition from the AKC.

When the Brindels gave up their kennels in Muncie, Indiana, and moved to Florida, Mr. Brindel became active in teaching obedience classes. They took their two favorite dogs with them, Sheba II de Belique and Francois de Chemin des Dames, or "Bing." Bing was in the pedigrees of many of the best Belgians in America at that time. The Brindels were not able to finish his championship because he was hit by a car, which left him lame. He was an excellent guard dog at their home. Mr. Brindel told an amusing story about a stranger approaching their house and meeting the big black dog blocking the entrance. The man tried to kick him out of the way. Bing caught his foot and set him down hard, then barked until Mr. Brindel told him it was all right.

The Brindels did not resume their breeding of Belgians after moving to Florida, but remained great boosters of the breed.

Mildred Shepard got her first Belgian Sheepdog from the Brindels in the forties. She was a charter member of the reorganized BSCA and remained active in the club until recently. Many fine dogs came from her Shady Lawn Kennels. Mildred was Second Vice President of the first Board of Directors in 1947.

Several sanctioned matches were held at the Shepard farm in Delphi, Indiana.

A few of her dogs were Ch. Ginger de Beaute Noir, Duke Prince, Ch. Black Bond, Etoile of Muncietta, and Contessa Becu du Barry.

Mr. and Mrs. Cecil Lutz lived in Pennsylvania. In 1945, Mrs. Lutz imported several Belgian Sheepdogs, and it was through her efforts that the Arthur Brindels and Myron Rowlands became interested in the breed. The Brindels got their Francois du Chemin des Dames and Sheba II de Belique from the Lutzes.

Mr. Lutz was a member of the first Board of Directors in 1947. The Lutzes were active breeders but their records have been lost over the years.

Mr. A. F. Goris, of Long Island, New York, imported three dogs after World War I. He went to Europe and selected three more after World War II. Two of the dogs he imported were Moto du Mont Sara, and Minora. Mr. Goris' kennel name was Beldome.

Mr. Goris was not a charter member, but he was an active breeder and exhibitor. Like those of some of the other old breeders, his kennel records and pictures have been lost.

All members from the early days contributed their efforts toward bringing the breed back into recognition when interest waned after the demise of the first BSCA. It was the opinion of many of the older breeders that Belgians were used in police work to such an extent at that time that people began to associate them more with that type of work and did not trust them as family dogs. It took many years to dispel this image.

In 1950 Belgian Sheepdogs started their upward swing in Group placements. Throughout the ensuing years they have continued their success in Group and Best in Show awards. The breed has come a long way since the first Belgian came to a strange new country, unknown and unheralded, with only his beauty to recommend him.

Afterword

How I Got Started

Rudy Robinson had been very impressed with the outstanding Zordoff, the "Champion of Italy." This dog represented the best of European lines from Switzerland, Belgium, France, and Italy. Robinson wanted to buy this sire to improve the breed in the United States, but he was not for sale. The breeder, Mr. Colombo, was of such high integrity that he wanted to be sure to ship the best specimen of Zordoff's litter, however. To accomplish that, he sent the entire litter so Robinson could see them all and make his own choice. All of the puppies in that litter were excellent; it was an overall good litter, both in body formation and temperament. They weren't shy and weren't aggressive. They all had beautiful coats and good teeth. Two of the best were Ch. Tazir III del Pirata Nero, owned by Ted and Freda Rowland of Roll In Kennels, and Ch. Liza del Pirata Nero, CD, who became the matriarch of my Geier Tal line. Liza loved to show in conformation. She enjoyed that and was a great one for baiting off another handler who was baiting his own dog. Most Belgians really like obedience, and in obedience Liza did everything right. However, she insisted on doing it at her own pace.

Breeding Concerns

One thing that has concerned me about type is that some of the Belgian heads have become too fine and too narrow. In some parts of the country, people have inbred too closely. They have ended up with smaller dogs, as well as running into other problems. You can also find temperament problems with too close a breeding. I did do one close breeding, but I had a purpose, and that was was to be sure that I knew what I had. I had been in dogs for quite some time and knew what I was looking for.

Anytime there is too much popularity in a breed and a lot of neighborhood breeding, you will find less quality because people who are not knowledgeable about the breed just use the nearest dog for breeding.

Belgians Today

I think when you look at all that Belgian Sheepdogs have accomplished, you have to conclude that the intelligence and temperament of the breed have improved overall. These days, more than ever, it is not enough to be just a champion. Belgian breeders want a dog that can work and play and be a true companion.

The all-time top-producing sire of champions, Triple BSCA BIS Ch. Rolin Ridge's Fourteen Karat, CD, HIC, HOF, ROM. He went Best in Show at the Belgian Sheepdog Club of America in 1987, 1991, and 1992, and Best of Breed and Group III at Westminster Kennel Club in 1991. Fourteen Karat was bred, owned, and handled by Linda M. McCarty. Photo © Cott.

APPENDIX A

BELGIAN SHEEPDOG CLUB OF AMERICA AWARDS
Requirements 2000

REGISTRY OF MERIT

The Registry of Merit (ROM) is a BSCA award based on offspring, not second generation progeny. For a sire to earn his ROM, he must have ten champion offspring, two advanced performance titled offspring, and a total of 100 points. The requirements for a dam are five champions, two advanced performance titled offspring, and a total of 50 points. The sire or dam must be an AKC Champion and must have at least a Companion Dog title (CD).

Advanced performance titles are as follows:
CDX and above
OA/OAJ and above
TD and above or
HS and above.

(No points are awarded for Canine Good Citizen (CGC), Endurance or Temperament Tests.)

1. The Belgian Sheepdog is an AKC Champion and Companion Dog. By the year 2001, dogs and bitches applying for the ROM are recommended to have OFA hips and elbows and CERF registrations.

2. As a sire, the dog has earned at least 100 points and the bitch has earned at least 50 points, based on the following point schedule:
   - Each Champion offspring merits 5 points.
   - Each Obedience titled offspring merits 5 points for each title earned.
   - Each Agility titled offspring merits 5 points for each title earned.

3. At least 10 offspring of the sire and 5 offspring of the dam must be Champions.

4. For both the sire and dam, at least 2 of the offspring must have either an advanced obedience degree (CDX, UD, UDX); an advanced agility title (OA/OAJ, AX/AXJ, MX/MXJ); an advanced herding title (HS, HI HX); or an advanced Tracking Title (TD, TDX or VST).

5. Points shall also be awarded for the following titled or certified offspring. (Points will *not* be granted for titles which duplicate existing AKC titles, but as separate titles, they will be granted equivalent points):
   a) AKC titles only unless you are a BSCA member from Canada, Mexico, or other foreign country.
   b) Schutzhund I, II, III–5 points each upon receipt of copy of certificate from a recognized Schutzhund organization.
   c) Service Dogs/Assistance Dogs to include Guide Dogs for the Blind/Police Dogs/Dogs for the Disabled, certified through an accredited agency–15 points.

d) Herding Dogs as follows:

AKC Titles:
AKC Pre-trial Tested (PT) shall be worth 5 points and shall count as a basic title.
Pre-trial Tested plus any other basic title, such as CD, TD or NA, shall count as an advanced title.
AKC Herding Tested (HT), Herding Instinct Certificate (HIC), and Herding Capability Test (HCT) shall not count towards the ROM requirements.

Australian Shepherd Club of America (ASCA) Herding Titles:
ASCA Started Trial Dog (STD) shall be considered equivalent to the AKC PT. STD titles shall count as 5 points and as a basic title.
ASCA Open Trial Dog (OTD) and Advanced Trial Dog (ATD) shall count 5 points and shall count as advanced titles.

American Herding Breed Association (AHBA) Titles prior to 7/1/91:
Junior Herding Dog (JHD) shall count as 5 points and count as a basic title.
AHBA Herding Trial Dog (HTD-I, II, III) shall count as 5 points and shall count as advanced titles.
Herding Ranch Dog (HRD-I, II, III) shall count as 5 points and shall count as advanced titles.

Duplicate titles with different types of stock shall not count for the ROM.

HALL OF FAME AWARDS

These national club awards are based on the performance of the dog, not his or her offspring. Hall of Fame awards are offered in three performance areas: obedience, breed, and working. Working Hall of Fame awards include obedience, tracking, agility, herding and service work.

Obedience

To qualify for the Obedience Hall of Fame, a dog or bitch must meet one of the following requirements:

- Dog or bitch must have a UD
- Dog or bitch must have 5 UDX legs
- Dog or bitch must accumulate 100 points under the following point system (AKC titles only unless member resides in a foreign country):

5 points each..........................CD, CDX
10 points..UD
15 points......................................UDX
20 points ....OTCH
Open or Utility Placements (A or B classes)
    10 points..................... 1st place
    8 points......................2nd place
    6 points....................... 3rd place
    4 points....................... 4th place
20 points............All breed High in Trial
    (all classes included)
15 points.........National Specialty High in Trial (all classes included)

Breed

This award is for achievement in the breed ring at AKC shows. Males must earn 150 points and 75 points are required for bitches. (Foreign group placements or foreign specialties wins do not count toward the total.)

Point Scale:
    20 points........................All-breed BIS Win
    20 points.........National Specialty BIS Win
    15 points...............National Specialty BOS
    5 points...............National Specialty Select
    10 points..............Area Specialty BOB Win
    8 points........................Area Specialty BOS
    10 points........................Herding Group I
    8 points..........................Herding Group II
    6 points........................Herding Group III
    4 points........................Herding Group IV

Working Dog

Working Dog Competition (WD-C) requires 5 points in 2 or more venues with one venue being 3 points or more.

Working Dog Excellent (WDX-C) requires 7 points in 2 or more venues with one venue being 3 points or more. (Note: In Agility you can count either standard class or jumpers, but not both.)

Working Dog/Service (WD-S)

Option 1: Certified Assistance Dog which has been in service for one year; including, but not limited to, Working Guide, Hearing, Service, Rescue or Police Dog. Submitted notarized certification from the service organization and the owner/handler. Acceptable service organizations include, but are not limited to, Guide Dogs for the Blind, Seeing Eye, Canine Companions for Independence, US Police Canine Association, Paws with a Cause, and other approved incorporated groups or chartered public agencies with written standards. A member may request that an organization and/or individual submit guidelines to the Working Dog Committee for approval.

Option 2: Working Herd Dog which does actual work on a regular basis. Submitted notarized certification from the rancher, farmer, owner, veterinarian, or other authorized person. Also submit a description of the dog's daily activities and any unusual or special activities that occurred while in service. A video would be accepted and encouraged.

Points Awarded Toward Working Dog Competition

Points	1	2	3	4	5
Agility	NA/NAJ	OA/OAJ	AX/AXJ	MX/MXJ	MACH
Obedience	CD	CDX	UD	UDX	OTCH
Tracking	—	TD	TDX	VST	TCH
Herding	PT	HS	HI	HX	HCH

Ch. La Neige's First Prototype, bred by Patricia J. Snow and owned by Joshua A. Clyborne and Shawn Clute.

APPENDIX B

RECENT BSCA AWARD WINNERS

Compiled by Lynn Sharkey

FOR THE YEAR 1999

Registry of Merit

Ch. Avatar Viva of Chez Les Bel, CDX
    Breeder/owners: Kathy and Jim
        Herman and Barbara Swisher

Breed Hall of Fame

Ch. Sumerwynd's Dana of Isengard, CDX, TD, HI, AX, AXJ
    Breeder: Dennette Cockley
    Owner: Lorra A. Miller

Select Am/Can SKC/Int. Ch. Johnson-dale's Sweet Sarana, CD, HIC, TT, CGC, TDI
    Breeder: Pat Johnson
    Owners: Sheila Martin and Cheryl Mallonee

Working Dog

Ch. Shalyn's Do You Wanna Dance, CD MX, MXJ
    Breeder/owner: Lynn Sharkey

Ch. Johnsondale's Pascha Partout, UD, HS
    Breeder: Pat Johnson
    Owner: Cathy Vella

Kupenda's Mahali Wakati Beti, CD, PT, AX, AXJ, SCh-B, U-CD, TDI, CGC
    Breeder: Sonja Ostrom
    Owner: Chris Libs

Ch. Reverie Hocuspocus, CDX, AX, OAJ
    Breeder: Jill A. Miller
    Owners: Gail and Tim O'Neil

Working Dog Excellent

Ch. Sumerwynd's Dana of Isengard, CDX, TD, HI, AX, AXJ
    Breeder: Dennette Cockley
    Owner: Lorra A. Miller

OTCh Licket's Tczar Kachina Doll, UDX, HS, OA, NAJ
    Breeder: Beth Lachnitt
    Owner: Tami Worley

Ch. Rodan De La Maison DuBois, UD, HS, OA OAJ
    Breeder: Madame Heraly
    Owner: Tami Worley

Obedience Hall of Fame

OTCh Licket's Tczar Kachina Doll, UDX, HS, OA, NAJ
    Breeder: Beth Lachnitt
    Owner: Tami Worley

FOR THE YEAR 2000

Registry of Merit

Ch. Reverie's Black Tie Affair, CD
  Owner: Jill Miller
  Breeders: Jill Miller, Millard and Jeani Brown, and K. Gangi

Ch. Liswyn's Candlefire of Geka, UDX
  Breeders: Lisa Leffingwell and Dottie Lee
  Owner: Lisa Leffingwell

BISS Ch. Rolin Ridge's Cameo, CD, HOF
  Breeder: Charlene Mascuch
  Owner: Linda McCarty

Breed Hall of Fame

Ch. Black Gold City Slicker
  Owner: Jane Waddle

Ch. SumerWynd Eye Spy TT
  Owner: Dennette Cockley

Ch. BelRoyale Cara O'Morningstar HS
  Owner: Joan Dyke

Ch. Sandcastle's Kutting Edge CD HT
  Owners: Sandra Shaw and David and Dottie Butler

Working Dog

Ushi Du Pre Du Vieux Pont, HS, MX, MXJ
  Owner: Elaine Havens

Ch. Blak Jak's Danseuse Du Soir, CD, MX, AXJ
  Owner: Rosie Lerner

Bris Natasha of Lascaux, CD, TDX, PT, NA, NAJ
  Owner: Wendy Sommer

Cassy's Fantasia De La Fusee, CD, MX, MXJ
  Owner: Sharon Lafuse

BSCA BIS Ch. Rolin Ridge's Cameo, HOF, was BIS at the 1993 Belgian Sheepdog Club of America Specialty and the 1994 Trinity Valley Belgian Sheepdog Club show. Bred by C. Mascuch, he was owned and handled by Linda McCarty. Photo © Orin Trademan.

Ch. Image's Award of Malachi, CD, JHD, PT, OA, AXJ
   Owners: Viola Dyer and Renee Croft

Working Dog Excellent

Ch. Bayview's Itza Queen's Game, UD, MX
   Owner: Linda Brady

Ch. Bris's Speedo From Sturgis, CDX, TDX, HS
   Owner: Wendy Sommer

Obedience Hall of Fame

Ch. Liswyn's Candlefire of Geka ,UDX
   Owner: Lisa Leffingwell

Ch. Rodan De La Masion Dubois, UD, HS, OA, OAJ
   Owner: Tami Worley

FOR THE YEAR 2001

Breed Hall of Fame

Ch. Bel-Reve's Y-Yatt Earp
   Owners/breeders: Cathy H. and William G. Daugherty

BIS/BISS Am. Can. Ch. Sans Branco Make My Day Cibola, TT
   Owners: Melinda Andric, Rhonda Smiley, and Terri Votava

Working Dog/Service

Certified Assistance Dog
Amblin's Enjoy the Moment, AX, AXJ, HIC
   Breeder: Allison James and Linda Brady
   Owners: Linda Brady and JoAnn Stuart
   Handler: JoAnn Stuart

Working Herd Dog

Ch. Cara Mia De Loup Noir, HX, CD, CGC, TDI
   Breeder: Steven Szabo
   Owners: Steven and Julia Szabo

Registry of Merit

Ch. Sundown's Phoenix Masquerade, CD, HIC, TT
   Breeder: Mike and Marcy Fine
   Owner: Lynn C. South

Ch. Liswyn's Firefly of Geka, UD
   Breeders: Lisa Leffingwell & Dottie Lee
   Owner: Lisa Leffingwell

Am. Can. Ch. Johnsondale's Windsong, CD, HIC, HOF
   Breeder: Pat Johnson
   Owner: Dennette Cockley

Ch. Johnsondale's I of the Storm, CD, TT, HIC, CGC
   Breeders: Pat Johnson and Shery Alligood
   Owner: Edgardo Simone

Ch. Starwind's Aquila of Kaori, HS, CD
   Breeders: Janice Handlers and Sharon Cochran
   Owners: Janice Handlers and Peri Norman

Working Dog

Ch. Liswyn's Havena Good Time, UD, AX, AXJ
   Owners: Sue Bonness and Gayle York

Ch. Rolin Ridge's Pepsi Please, TD, HIA-s
   Owners: Mr. and Mrs. C.D. Goddard

Ch. Sherborne Zola Ban'd n Bostn, UD, PT, NA
   Owner: Lynnette Gandl

Rolin Ridge's Proud Promise, CDX, OA, AXJ
   Owner: Mary Lynn Butcher

Celebre Drastic Action, HSA-d, AX, OAJ
  Owner: Ann B. Johnstone

Ch. Discovery's Great Escape, CD, MX, MXJ, HIC
  Owner: Linda Brady

Ch. Discovery's Bayview Gossip, CDX, AX, AXJ
  Owners: Karen Hodges and Linda Brady

Ch. Cara Mia De Loup Noir, HX, CD, CGC, TDI
  Owners: Steven and Julia Szabo

Working Dog Excellent

Ch. Rolin Ridge's Pathfinder, TD, HXA-s, HSB-s, NA
  Owners: Mr. and Mrs. Charles D. Goddard

Ch. Meadowyn's A'int She Sweet, VCD2, PT, AX, AXJ
  Owner: Joanne E. Kutsch

Ch. Inselheim Charfire Shandar, UD, HX
  Owners: Janice Handlers and Elaine Havens

Obedience Hall of Fame

Ch. Legacy's Keep a Secret Sophia, UDX
  Owner: Wendy Reese

Cassidy V Siegestor, UDX
  Owner: Charlene T. Vincent

Agility Hall of Fame

Ch. MACH2 Shalyn Dances on Heir
  Owners: Kurt and Jean Matushek

Mawrmyth's Kokopelli, HT, MX, MXJ
  Owners: Carol Tacquard and Marcy Spalding

Ch. Discovery's Great Escape, CD, MX, MXJ, HIC
  Owner: Linda Brady

Ch. Sumerwynd's Dana of Isengard, VCD2, HS, HI, HXA-d, MX, AXJ
  Owner: Lorra Miller

Ch. Shalyn's Do You Wanna Dance, CD, MX, MXJ
  Owner: Lynn Sharkey

Cassy's Fantasia of De LaFuse, CD, MX, MXJ
  Owner: Sharon LaFuse

Ch. Sandcastle's Kutting Edge, CD, HT, CGC, won multiple Best In Specialty shows, Group wins, and High in Trials (obedience).
In 1999 he was nationally ranked as the No. 1 Belgian Sheepdog, and in 2001 he was nationally ranked as No. 1 all breeds.

Ch. Belle Noire Laxson du Jet, CDX, TT, "Jean Jean," at thirteen months. Owner, Kaye Hall.

Other Sources of Information

CLUBS

Belgian Sheepdog Club of America (BSCA)
www.bsca.info/home

Carol Morris, BSCA Corresponding Secretary
8315 Cave City Road
Mountain Ranch, CA 95246

Paul Ponzio Jr., BSCA Rescue Chairperson
www.bsca.info/rescue

Belgian Sheepdog Club of Canada (BSCC)
www.geocities.com/Heartland/Estates/2410

American Kennel Club (AKC)
5580 Centerview Rd.
Raleigh, NC 27606
(919) 239-9767
www.akc.org

HEALTH ORGANIZATIONS

Orthopedic Foundation for Animals (OFA)
2300 E. Nifong Blvd.
Columbia, MO 65201
www.ofa.org

Canine Eye Registration Foundation
Purdue University
1235 South Campus Courts, Building A
West Layayette, IN 47907
www.vet.purdue.edu/%7Eyshen/cerf

OTHER ACTIVITIES:

Agility Association
P.O. Box 850955
Richardson, TX 75085-0955
www.usdaa.com

Search and Rescue Organization (SAR)
P.O. Box 3709
Fairfax, VA 22038
(703) 252-1349

The American Herding Breed Association (AHBA)
c/o Carol Lorenzon
3767 W. 136th St.
Cleveland, OH 44111
(216) 941-6330
www.ahba-herding.org/index.htm

The North American Flyball Association (NAFA)
P.O. Box 8, Mount Hope
Ontario, Canada L0R 1W0
www.flyball.org

United Schutzhund Clubs of America
3810 Paule Ave.
St. Louis, MO 63125
(314) 638-0609

Therapy Dog International (TDI)
6 Hilltop Rd.
Mendham, NJ 07945
(908) 429-0670
www.tdi-dog.org

PUBLICATIONS

BSCA Breeders Directory
www.bsca.info/BreedersDirectory

BSCA Puppy Manual
www.bsca.info/BSCApuppymanual

Belgians From Start to Finished
(covers all Belgian breeds)
Sally Ann Comstock
1997, Beyond Graphics, Maumelle, AK
(To be reprinted 2003 by Alpine Publications, Loveland, CO)

Belgian Sheepdogs Video
20 min. VHS
American Kennel Club, New York, NY

The National Belgian Newsletter
published by the Belgian Sheepdog Club of America, Inc.
(Contact current treasurer to subscribe. *See* AKC website, herding breeds.)

TRIBUTE TO THE AUTHOR

Marge Turnquist passed away on December 20, 2002. This edition of the book was completed just before her death, with the dedicated assistance of Carolyn Hackney. Marge will be sorely missed by many in the fancy, and she was greatly admired by friends and associates. Following are some of the tributes written shortly after her death:

It is always hard to lose a friend, and sometimes it is more than just a personal loss—it is a loss to the whole world of dogs. . . . Marge wrote the main treatise on the Belgian Sheepdog, the big red book that we all know (the first edition of this book) and served on the BSCA board. I had the pleasure of serving with Marge in her later years, and I valued our correspondence. The dogs were never far from her mind and memory.

Sonja Ostrom

A true friend is hard to find, but Marge has been just that to me since 1955. She was my mentor. She knew more about Belgians than anyone I know. At the time I started in the breed, her dogs were the best in the "country, bar none. She used to say, "No shoulder, no Belgian." We have lost a true advocate of the breed and a true lover of dogs.

Sheila Rentschler

Marge loved puppies. Once when we asked her to evaluate some young Belgians, we merely sat out in the yard and watched them. Rather than trying to examine wiggly puppies, she preferred to watch them move naturally as they played. From time to time she commented that one had made some nice moves, or another had struck a good pose. It was not a hurried event—just a time to enjoy being with the puppies.

There was much more to Marge than just her dogs, although they were a large part of her life. She hand painted porcelain with various subjects and seasons. She obedience trained some of her Belgians and many of her Shepherds, working right alongside her husband, Ed.

After Marge's last Belgian died, she wasn't sure whether she wanted another dog. Then Casey came along. He was an older German Shepherd puppy that some friends found being mistreated. He was still friendly and trusting so Marge bought him from his junk yard owner, rescuing the puppy and finding her last companion. When she was hospitalized in July 2002, it was the first time she was not able to return to her beloved Casey. She needed rehabilitation and went, temporarily we thought, to a nursing home. There she quickly made friends with the nurses and staff. For her birthday in November, they gave her a bobble-headed German Shepherd that she kept by her bed because it reminded her of Casey. Marge was walking very well again and appeared to be much improved in December. She wanted to go home, watch her birds through the window and have Casey by her side. It was not to happen.

We will not soon forget Marge—her outspokenness, her concern and consideration for others and her dogs. She helped and encouraged so many. She was from a time when exhibitors were friends who encouraged one another and didn't mind sharing the wins. We can all learn a great deal from her example.

Carolyn Hackney